POPS!

POPS!

ICY TREATS FOR EVERYONE

Krystina Castella

QUIRK BOOKS

PHILADELPHIA

Library of Congress Cataloging-in-Publication Number: 2007941761

ISBN: 978-1-59474-253-8

Printed in China

Typeset in Eureka Sans and Compatil Fact

A Quirk Packaging Book
Designed by Niloo Tehranchi
Illustrations on pages 118–125 by Stislow Design + Illustration

10 9 8 7 6 5

Quirk Books
215 Church Street
Philadelphia, PA 19106
quirkbooks.com

FOR MY PHENOMENAL HUSBAND, BRIAN BOYL:
Thanks for chillin' with me.

ACKNOWLEDGMENTS

Thank you to everyone on Team *Pops!*

Countless thank yous to **Sarah Scheffel,** project editor and Team *Pops!* editorial director, whose imagination and insight have made crafting *Pops!* all play.

Team *Pops!* Los Angeles
Emily Brooke Sandor: the photographer whose commitment and hard work from concept to final book gave form to these cool images.
Liesl Maggiore: the food stylist whose good humor kept us from dripping.
Glendale Department of Water and Power: who saved the pops during a blackout by donating a backup generator so the photo shoot could go on.

Team *Pops!* New York: Quirk Packaging
Lynne Yeamans: the design director who infused her playful vision into these pages.
Liana Krissoff: the recipe editor who tackled every last detail.
Niloo Tehranchi: the graphic designer who brought her impeccable style to every page.
Sharyn Rosart: the book packager who agreed to pull off *Pops!* lickety-split.

Team *Pops!* Philadelphia: Quirk Books
Mindy Brown: the associate publisher whose availability as a sounding board brought a clear understanding and vision to this book.
Dave Borgenicht: the publisher who agreed to back Project *Pops!* and set us off on an adventure of a lifetime.
Melissa Wagner: the acquisitions editor, for her creative direction and for acquiring *Pops!* within forty-five minutes of receiving the proposal.
Bryn Ashburn: the art director, for her discerning eye.

And to my parents, **Marion and Michael Castella,** for their invaluable support.

CONTENTS

FRUIT JUICE POPS

Ingredients are mixed and frozen 41

2

HEALTHY ENERGY POPS

Ingredients are blended and frozen 23

1

SODA FOUNTAIN POPS

Based on soda floats and ice cream treats 57

3

CREAM AND PUDDING POPS

Made from cream, yogurt, and pudding bases 73

4

COCKTAIL POPS

Based on mixed, blended, and frozen cocktails 103

6

COFFEE AND TEA POPS

Based on international coffee and tea drinks 87

5

POP OBSESSED!

When I was eight years old, my mom attended a Tupperware party and surprised me by bringing home a special treat: ice pop molds. At first I found it a little strange that grown-ups had fun at parties that celebrated plastic products. But when we made strawberry and orange ice pops using orange juice and fresh strawberries I'd grown in our garden it hit me: It wasn't about the plastic but the possibilities the voids in the molds held. I also realized I wouldn't have to eagerly wait until 2:15 every day for my favorite melody coming from the ice cream truck, then beg my parents for fifty cents to buy my favorite icy treat. I was being encouraged to make and eat pops all the time. The ice cream man could live in our freezer!

I poured everything I could think of into the molds—juice, ice cream, pudding, yogurt, candy, fruit, nuts—and through freezing transformed them. To me everything tasted better frozen on a stick—especially in New York City in summertime. When we learned about the science of freezing in third grade, I jumped up and gave a speech about all I'd learned from making ice pops. Throughout my teens I made them as a healthy alternative to ice cream. In college I studied industrial design, a major that allowed me to explore plastics and mold-making techniques to feed my pops obsession.

Ice pops even played a central role in my romantic life. I was eating a pop when the phone rang one day. It was Brian, a guy I'd met at a party the night before, calling to ask me out on our first date. I was so excited I quickly wrapped my pop up in foil and parked it in the freezer so we could talk. Throughout our five years of dating, every time I moved I packed the same ice pop in an ice cooler and refroze it at my new place, as a quirky good luck token for our relationship. Several years ago, about the time of our tenth wedding anniversary, I decided it was time to say goodbye to that freezer-burnt pop and hello to a whole new world of specialty pops.

With the numerous innovative plastic and silicone molds on the market, I discovered I could make ice pops that offer unusual forms as well as unique flavor combinations. I could finally make ice pops that were glistening, tasty, beautiful objects of art. And as an industrial designer equipped with mold-making skills, I could make custom molds in almost any shape I dreamed of—just like toys.

After the success of my cookbook *Crazy about Cupcakes* (crazyaboutcupcakes.com), I decided to write about the next fun, fashionable food: ice pops, of course. Partly because I had a lifetime of pop making under my belt, but also because these childhood favorites are a perfect reminder for us all to approach life with playfulness, wonder, and a sense of humor, pops seemed like the ideal follow-up. Just like cupcakes, pops are fun and make people smile.

Ice pops also fit into a larger cultural trend. "Kidults" who spend their weekends hanging out at cupcake bakeries, shopping for collectible toys, and creating DIY crafts or tech projects will enjoy the creative opportunities that playing in the kitchen and making pops offers. They will be proud to serve these hand-crafted homemade treats at their formerly too-adult birthdays, barbecues, and cocktail parties. Moms and dads who store these delicious treats in the freezer for their kids will be treated like heroes. Kids and teens will find these recipes cool and easy to make for their friends. And the health conscious looking for completely fat-free after-workout frozen delights will find many pops that meet their healthy requirements and satisfy their palates, too. To expand your taste for icy treats, I also have included recipes for global ices from around the world.

The recipes and techniques in *Pops! Icy Treats for Everyone* are a compilation of many years of testing flavors and shapes, experimenting with texture, and developing innovative freezing and mold-making techniques. My hope is that this book will encourage you to have fun creating pops that are uniquely your own. As a simple treat on a hot summer afternoon or an elegant finish to a special meal, ice pops can be as casual or fancy and as healthful or indulgent as you choose!

Krystina Castella
Glendale, CA

icypops.com
kcastella@msn.com

POPS CULTURE:
How to Say Ice Pop

English: Ice pop (US and Canada), ice lolly (UK), ice block or ice pole (Australia and New Zealand)

American Sign Language: Move hand up to mouth as if licking an ice pop

French: *Glace à l'eau*

German: *Eis am stiel*

Italian: *Ghiacciolo*

Spanish: *Polo o paleta de helado, paleta*

Portuguese: *Picolé*

Swedish: *Isglasspinne*

Danish: *Sodavandsis*

Chinese: *Bing tiau*

Farsi: *Bastani choobee*

Korean: *Ice keki*

Japanese: *Ice poppu*

ICE POP INGREDIENTS: From Bases to Toppings to Hidden Surprises

You can make ice pops from almost any ingredient you choose, but there are some things you need to know to ensure successful pops. All ingredients are not alike when it comes to freezing. One general principle to consider is that the further away the ingredient is from the purity of water, the lower the freezing point and the longer it will take to freeze. Another is that sugar lowers the freezing point of ingredients and keeps the base molecules from sticking together and forming hard blocks of ice. Dissolving the sugar in the base in-gredient will create pops with a nice, smooth texture, and will allow the flavors to be distributed evenly throughout the pop.

Since all ingredients will expand while freezing, leave at least ¼ inch of space at the top of the molds when filling them. Liquid ingredients that have high air content, such as sodas and smoothies, will expand more than solid ingredients such as pudding and yogurt.

BASES

Juices and Smoothies: The natural sugars in fruit juices produce pops with a smooth texture. The easiest and quickest option is to use good-quality store-bought juices, but you can expand your options by making fresh homemade juice from pure fruit. Use a juicer, or smash or puree the fruit in a blender and pass it through a fine-mesh sieve or a colander lined with rinsed and squeezed cheesecloth.

Smoothies are made from blending juices, sugar, and whole fruit in a food processor or blender, and their thickness makes them the perfect base if you want to suspend and distribute fruit evenly in your pops.

Yogurt, Pudding, and Gelatin: Freezing yogurt is a healthier alternative to store-bought frozen yogurt, which typically contains a lot of sugar and other additives. Yogurt is alive. When you freeze it, the healthy cultures become dormant, but once they're ingested they come back to life.

I call pudding and gelatin pops "wonder pops" because they don't drip or melt too quickly and can be savored for a long time. Pops based on juices, smoothies, coffee, and tea can be made into wonder pops by adding unflavored gelatin to the mixture. The thickness of yogurt, pudding, and gelatin makes them good bases in which to suspend mix-ins. For easy removal, use flexible or disposable molds when you make pops with a yogurt, pudding, or gelatin base.

JUICE POP   **YOGURT POP**

Coffee and Tea: If you prefer strong coffee and tea, brew these pop bases twice as strong as you would if you were drinking them hot, because freezing dulls the taste. Coffee and tea have a high water content, so pops made with them will be harder and stay icy longer than other pops. Add milk and sugar to smooth out the texture. Allow coffee and tea to cool slightly in the refrigerator before placing the pops in the freezer.

Ice Cream, Sherbet, and Frozen Yogurt: Any store-bought ice cream, sherbet, and frozen yogurt can be formed into pops. Allow ice cream to soften slightly before packing it into the molds. Dense, harder ice creams (usually the more expensive brands) with less air are easier to mold, but ice creams with less fat (usually the cheaper brands) stay on the stick better.

Ice cream, sherbet, and frozen yogurt can also be cut into squares or circles depending on the shape of the container. Cookie cutters can also be used to form shapes. First peel off the paper container. With a large knife or cookie cutter, create pop-size pieces. Insert the stick and place on waxed paper on a cookie sheet or stand them up in a piece of Styrofoam. Cover with plastic wrap or plastic bags and refreeze.

Homemade ice cream can also be frozen into pops. The advantage of creating pops with homemade ice cream is that before the ice cream becomes solid you can pour the slushy liquid into the pop molds—which is easier than packing solid ice cream into molds. For easy removal, use flexible or disposable molds for pops made with ice cream, sherbet, or frozen yogurt bases.

Pop Tips

HOW TO MAKE PERFECT POPS
- Always use the freshest ingredients.
- Clear just enough space in the freezer.
- Pour ingredients into molds from spouted containers.
- Prepare ahead and allow plenty of freezing time.
- Keep the pops in the molds as long as possible.
- If the pops are not in molds, cover them with plastic wrap or baggies.
- Substitute ingredients to create your own pops.

SHERBET POP   **TEA POP**

ALCOHOL POPS

Alcoholic Beverages: Alcohol freezes at a much lower temperature than water—as low as –173 degrees F (–114 C) depending on the proof. Most home freezers don't go this low. The key to making pops with alcohol is to use a relatively small amount of alcohol mixed with other ingredients. The other ingredients will freeze solid, and the alcohol will be suspended within the other molecules. However, there are a couple ways to get more alcohol content into a pop:

- Put pieces of fruit, cookies, or cake in a small bowl with the alcohol and let them soak for 10 minutes before using them in pop recipes. Fruits with large pores and low juice content, such as apples and pears, will absorb alcohol better than juicier fruits.
- Mix alcohol with a bit of light corn syrup or simple syrup (see page 113) and put the mixture in the freezer for about 1 hour, or until very cold but not frozen. Dip the frozen pop in the mixture and serve immediately or refreeze.

MIX-INS, TOPPINGS, AND HIDDEN SURPRISES

Mix-ins: Mixing fruit, nuts, candies, chips, seeds, and healthy boosters into the base flavors offers hundreds of variations of the same recipes. Try adding to some of these recipes by experimenting with new flavor combinations. When preparing 6 or 8 pops at a time, make each pop a different flavor by adding different ingredients to each pop mold, then pouring in the base mixture.

Toppings: Ingredients also can be used as toppings after the pop is frozen. Lighter toppings such as spices will stick right to the pop. For heavier toppings, like nuts or candies, first coat the pops with honey, corn syrup, or simple syrup (see page 113), then pat the topping onto the pop.

Hidden Surprises: Stick a chocolate-covered banana, a large chunk of pineapple, a cherry, or a caramel candy onto the pop stick before it is inserted into the pop mold and cleverly obscured by an opaque base mixture. See opposite for more ideas for mix-ins, toppings, and hidden surprises.

MIX-INS AND HIDDEN SURPRISES

MIX-AND-MATCH POPS INGREDIENTS

When it comes to ice pop flavors, let your imagination (and your taste buds) be your guide. Once you're familiar with the basic techniques in this book, you can create your own unique pops based on the recipes here. Choose a base recipe from the appropriate chapter, then substitute the flavors and color combinations you love. Here's a list of delicious ingredients to consider, but don't let it limit you: Want to create a caramel chocolate pop topped with salt sprinkles? Go for it. Or a bacon and waffle breakfast pop? Just be sure to email me the recipe if it works out.

1) CHOOSE ONE OR MORE BASES

Juices: apple and green apple, apricot nectar, blackberry, blueberry, blood orange and orange, carrot, cherry, coconut milk, cranberry, fruit punch, grape, guava nectar, lemon and lemonade, lime and limeade, mango nectar, papaya nectar, passion fruit, peach, pineapple, pink and yellow grapefruit, plum, pomegranate, raspberry, strawberry, tangerine, tomato, wheatgrass, white grape **Yogurts:** banana, berry, cherry, coconut, key lime, lemon, mango, orange, peach, pineapple, plain, raspberry, strawberry, vanilla **Puddings:** banana, butterscotch, chocolate, coconut custard, flan, Indian, lemon, persimmon, pistachio, quince, rice, vanilla, white chocolate **Gelatins:** apricot, cherry, cranberry, grape, lemon, lime, mixed fruit, orange, peach, pineapple, raspberry, strawberry, unflavored, watermelon **Coffees:** amaretto, Blue Mountain, caramel, chocolate, cinnamon, Colombian, Costa Rican, French roast, French vanilla, hazelnut, Irish cream, Kenyan, Kona, orange, raspberry, Sumatran **Teas:** apricot, black, black currant, blueberry, Ceylon, chai, chamomile, Darjeeling, Earl Grey, English breakfast, gingerbread, green, jasmine, Lapsang Souchong, lemon, mint, Oolong, orange pekoe, orange spice, peach, raspberry, strawberry, white **Ice creams, sherbets, and frozen yogurts:** bubble gum, butter pecan, chocolate, chocolate chip, coffee, cookie dough, cookies and cream, fudge swirl, lemon, lime, mango, maple walnut, mint, orange, peach, peanut butter, pistachio, pralines and cream, pumpkin, raspberry, rum raisin, strawberry, vanilla, vanilla fudge **Alcoholic beverages:** amaretto, blue curaçao, bourbon, brandy, Champagne, Cognac, gin, Grand Mariner, grenadine, Irish cream, Kahlúa, midori, orange curaçao, rum, schnapps, scotch, sherry, tequila, triple sec, vodka, vermouth, wine

2) CHOOSE MIX-INS AND TOPPINGS

Nuts: almonds, cashews, chestnuts, hazelnuts, peanuts, pecans, pine nuts, walnuts **Seeds:** caraway, fennel, poppy, pumpkin, sesame, sunflower **Coconut:** flaked or shredded **Crushed cookies:** chocolate sandwich cookies, gingersnaps, graham crackers, sugar cones, sugar wafers **Ground hard candy:** butterscotch, citrus, peppermint, root beer **Chopped chips and bits:** butterscotch, chocolate (white, milk, semisweet), cinnamon, mint, mint chocolate, peanut butter, peanut butter chocolate, toffee **Tiny candies:** cake decorator toppings, colored or chocolate sprinkles, nonpareils **Sugars:** colored or granulated **Spices:** allspice, chile, cinnamon, ginger, lemongrass, mint, nutmeg, salt **Zests:** lemon, lime, orange

ESSENTIAL ICE POP **TOOLS:** Freezers, Molds, and Sticks

THE FREEZER

There aren't many ways to make pops without a freezer unless you live in North Dakota or Alaska and it's winter. If your freezer is not working properly there will definitely be a meltdown. Understanding how to maximize your home freezer's potential will enable you to make successful pops.

Accurately controlling the freezer temperature is more difficult than setting an oven at a desired temperature. Adjust the dial in the freezer to the coldest temperature, around 0 degrees F (-18 C). Confirm the temperature by placing a thermometer in the freezer. Avoid opening the freezer often. When the freezer is opened, the cold air pours out and the freezer has to cool again.

Clear only as much space in the freezer as needed to fit the pop molds but still allow air to circulate around them. Filling the freezer with other frozen items helps to keep the freezer cooler longer, because the frozen food displaces air, so there is less air to cool. Freeze the pop molds in the coldest part of the freezer (usually the top shelf).

Patience is the key: Allow plenty of time for your pops to freeze. Different ingredients freeze at different rates. There is also a difference between freezing and freezing solid. In 6 to 8 hours, 6- and 8-ounce pops will be firm but not yet frozen solid. Smaller pops will take less time, and recipes with alcohol will take more time. Freezing overnight is a safe bet for most ingredients.

Keep the pops in their molds as long as possible to avoid freezer burn. Frozen pops left in their molds will stay fresh for 1 to 2 weeks. When freezing pops on a baking sheet, cover them with plastic wrap or aluminum foil. If freezing upright on a piece of Styrofoam, cover the pops with individual plastic baggies and secure with ties.

THE MOLDS

Designing and making pops is as much fun as eating them. Collecting and acquiring pop molds and ice cube trays has become my obsession. I love using unusual molds to create beautiful pops as delicious art objects. Sometimes I use single molds to layer and marbleize ingredient combinations within one pop mold. Other times I cast one pop in an ice cube tray or a smaller mold and then take that pop and put it into a larger mold to make a single pop with a shape inside. The possibilities are endless.

Selecting Manufactured Molds: Most molds on the market are one-part upright molds. The ingredients are poured from the top, and the stick caps off the mold. As you shop for pop molds, you will find a price and quality range. I have purchased pop molds in unique shapes for 99 cents and I have paid over $20 for a single pop mold. The most important feature to consider when shopping for molds is the draft angle: the greater the angle, the better. Hard plastic molds need at least a 3-degree angle from top to bottom (see the illustration on page 123) for the pop to be easily removed. Some cheaper molds have shallower angles, so you need to let the pop sit at room temperature for a few minutes before it can be removed from the mold. If the pop is too melted, it can detach from the stick and get stuck in the mold. Expensive molds tend to be made from more flexible plastic, are more durable, and are engineered better. However, there are many very good, well-designed, inexpensive molds on the market. Molds with detailed shapes, rockets, stars, and flowers are great additions to a pop mold collection.

Silicone molds are the most expensive, but they are very easy to use. The flexibility of silicone allows the pop to be removed from the mold immediately after it is removed from the freezer. There aren't many silicone pop molds on the market, but there are many silicone ice cube and baking trays that can be converted into pop molds (see page 120). And you can make your own silicone pop molds from any found or sculpted object (see page 123 for instructions).

Selecting Ice Cube Trays for Mini Pops: Ice cube trays are manufactured from either hard plastic or silicone rubber. Plastic trays are inexpensive, making it easy to convert several trays into pop molds to make dozens of pops for large parties. Pops made in silicone rubber trays can be taken out of the mold within seconds of being removed from the freezer. This is a fantastic feature, because mini ice pops are just that—small—and because they melt quickly, they need to be consumed more quickly. For more about converting ice cube trays to pop molds, see page 120.

Check out Do-It-Yourself Pop Molds on page 118 for lots of cool ideas for making your own pop molds from found objects and everyday household materials.

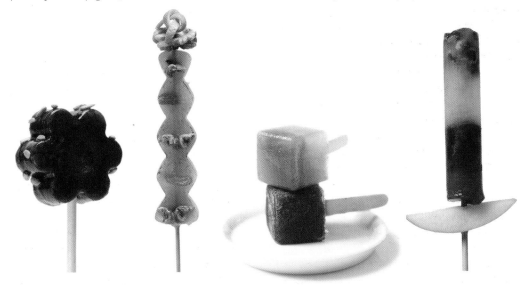

POP MOLDS COME IN MANY FUN SHAPES AND SIZES. YOU CAN ALSO MAKE YOUR OWN (SEE PAGE 118 FOR INSTRUCTIONS).

Ingredients and Molds: Thin mixtures, such as juices, coffees, and teas, can be cast into either hard plastic or silicone molds. Thicker mixtures, such as ice creams, yogurts, and puddings, are easier to remove from disposable molds (cups and packaging containers) and silicone molds.

THE STICKS

In my opinion, ice is not a pop until it has a stick. Sticks serve several functions. They prevent icy liquid from getting all over your hands. Sticks also come into play when pulling the pop out of the mold.

Ideally, the pop stick should have holes so that the ice can expand into the holes and grab onto the stick so it doesn't slip out. If possible, punch or drill holes into the pop ends of your sticks.

Traditional Pop Sticks: Traditional pop sticks made of basswood not only appeal to the nostalgia in all of us but also work very well. These sticks are light and durable, and the rounded edges make them safe to put in your mouth. The wood grain expands as the ice around it expands, making for a tight grip. Some vintage sticks found at flea markets and in online auctions are printed with fun sayings and surprises. You can make your own by decorating or writing on the stick with a food-safe marker and burying the image or phrase in the pop. Others have small toys on the end of the handle or hidden inside the pop. When making pops for adults, consider gluing toys to the pop sticks with nontoxic glue. (This is not recommended when making pops for children.)

Innovative Pop Sticks: There are many other items that can be used as pop sticks. I collect sticks of all sizes, shapes, and materials and try them out when making my pops.

Wooden coffee stirrers and bamboo barbecue skewers are available in different lengths. Just make sure that the sharp end is cut off before inserting one in the pop.

Plastic sticks are colorful and come in many shapes, but are a little more sensitive than wood. These will work best when using flexible or disposable molds so you don't need to pull with a lot of force to get the pops out of the molds. Plastic cocktail stirrers and cocktail picks are available in many colors, shapes, and sizes, and make great handles. They are reusable as well.

Pop Tips

KEEP YOUR STICKS STRAIGHT

- Use high-quality molds with sticks that snap onto the top of the mold and remain straight.
- Allow the pop to partially freeze for 15 to 30 minutes, then remove the mold from the freezer and insert the stick into the partially frozen pop.
- Cover the mold with aluminum foil and cut slits in the foil to support the stick.
- Create a custom durable lid for the mold to hold the sticks straight (see page 120).

POP STICK POSSIBILITIES
Cocktail stirrers
Cocktail picks (blunted)
Bamboo skewers (blunted)
Lollypop sticks
Rigid plastic straws (large boba straws,
     crazy straws)
Wooden coffee stirrers
Wooden dowels
Chopsticks
Acrylic rods and tubing
Light sticks
Plastic spoons

INNOVATIVE POP STICKS

ICE POP **TECHNIQUES:** Let's Get Fancy

You can make most of the pops in this book by mixing the ingredients together and freezing them in standard store-bought molds. But if you want to get fancy, here are a number of special techniques you can try. Examples of these techniques are shown in the photos throughout the book.

LAYERING

Layering Stripes: Freezing in layers is a great way to combine flavors and make colorful striped pops. Vertical molds create top-down stripes (see photo, opposite); horizontal molds create stripes from the front to back. Like ingredients stick together the best. For example, layering several types of puddings, or layering several types of juices, will work better than layering puddings with juices. Pour the layers into the mold as thick or thin as you like. (To create slanted stripes, tilt the mold by leaning it against the freezer wall.) Thin layers will take about 30 minutes to freeze, and thicker layers could take 1 hour or longer. The stick may not need to be inserted in the first few layers but when the depth where the stick begins is reached, set the stick in the partially frozen pop. Continue to freeze until firm, and fill the mold until full. Freeze the entire pop for 6 to 8 hours.

Suspending Ingredients: To suspend mix-ins, freeze ingredients in layers using either the same base or different bases. For example, when suspending berries in a juice pop, add one or two berries to the first layer and freeze. In the second layer in the middle of the pop, add more juice and a few more berries and freeze. Continue until the mold is full. (See photo, opposite.)

Layering from the Inside Out: Spread thicker ingredients like pudding or ice cream around the inside edge of the mold with a knife, leaving a hollow core. Freeze for 1 to 2 hours, until firm. If the mold is wide and you can create multiple layers, add another layer in the same way, leaving a smaller core. For the final interior core, use a pastry bag with tip insert (or a zip-top bag with the bottom corner cut off) to squeeze the final ingredient into the negative space. Insert the stick and freeze.

Marbleizing
Thicker ingredients, such as yogurt, pudding, and ice cream, can be stirred together to create swirl patterns. (See yogurt pop, page 10.) Gently stir two, three, or even four flavors together with a spoon in a bowl, then pour the mixture into pop molds. Another method is to combine the ingredients in a mold and then stir gently with a knife. Depending on the depth of the molds, you might want to add and mix the ingredients in several stages. Runny ingredients such as defrosted frozen berries will automatically marbleize the base ingredients with minimal stirring.

ICE CUBE INSERTS

I like to cast stars and hearts and other shapes in small molds or ice cube trays made from one pop mixture and then insert that shape into another semitransparent ingredient so the shape is visible from the outside. The interior shape could either be cast onto the end of the pop stick or floated in the base ingredients. To keep the interior shape from dissolving in the base ingredients, they must be frozen solid and placed into partially frozen base ingredients.

SUSPENDED INGREDIENTS   **LAYERING STRIPES**

How to Top Your Pop

Coatings, Heated
Chocolate: bars, chips
Fruit jam: add a little water to thin
Honey: add a little water to thin

Coatings, Unheated
Caramel
Spirits
Fruit juice
Maple syrup
Chocolate syrup
Marshmallow topping
Simple syrup (page 113)
Quick-hardening chocolate for ice cream

1. Prepare small shapes out of one pop mixture in ice cube trays and freeze until hard.
2. Partially freeze the base ingredient in larger pop molds.
3. When the base ingredient is partially frozen, insert the small shapes into the larger mold.
4. Freeze the entire pop for 6 to 8 hours.

HAND-DIPPED COATINGS

Pops taste heavenly encased in coatings such as caramel, fruit, and chocolate glaze. Hand dipping ice and ice cream pops is not as tricky as it seems. Thicker coatings, like chocolate, will need to be melted, while toppings like spirits can be used in their natural state. The secret here is to let the heated toppings cool slightly before dipping so they don't melt the

HAND-DIPPED COATINGS

pop. Work quickly to maximize their glaze potential. If the coating begins to harden, spread it with a knife and improvise by adding an additional layer of nuts, coconut, candy, or crushed cookies.

Thinner liquids, such as spirits, maple syrup, corn syrup, and juice can also be used to add additional flavor to the pop's surface. They can be used solely as a glaze, or lighter toppings, such as sugar, spices, or small seeds, can be added. To coat any of the pops in this book, you'll need:

> 1½ cups coating (see ideas, page 19)
> 1 cup topping (see mix-ins, page 13)

1. Prepare the pop recipe of your choice. Freeze for 6 hours.
2. If the coating needs to be melted, heat the coating in the top of a double boiler over simmering water. Stir constantly until thinned and just about melted. Remove from the heat and stir. Let cool for 8 to 10 minutes, to room temperature.
3. Remove a pop from the mold. Dip the pop into the coating until covered, allowing the excess to drip onto a plate. Sprinkle toppings over the coating. Press lightly with a knife to adhere. Repeat this process one at a time with the remaining pops. Serve.

If you will be storing the pops before you serve them, push the sticks into a block of Styrofoam, cover with individual plastic baggies secured with ties, and return them to the freezer.

How to Eat an Ice Pop

There isn't one right way to enjoy an ice pop. But here's a collection of tips from pop lovers I've encountered over the years.

- Stop what you're doing and relax.
- Start from the top of the pop and work your way down.
- Lick around the edges to avoid drips.
- Biting is okay—if you don't mind a little brain freeze.
- Focus on the final bite to keep the pop from sliding off the stick.
- Hold the stick with a napkin.
- Avoid getting covered in drips by holding the pop away from your body.
- Or let yourself get covered in drips and be reminded of the sticky messes you made as a kid.
- To cure an ice pop headache, simply press your tongue to the roof of your mouth until it subsides.

ICE POP PRESENTATION: How to Serve Dripless Pops with Style

GARNISHES

Garnish pop sticks with common drink garnish techniques. Some molds will allow sticks to pierce the pop from the top and the bottom, allowing for garnishes at both ends. Prepare all of the garnishes ahead of time and have them waiting when the pops are complete. Attach fruits, zests, or vegetables to the stick immediately before serving. Some garnishes can be skewered onto the stick; others are best tied to the stick. If you prefer, drill a hole in the stick before freezing the pop and insert the garnish into the hole.

SERVING SUGGESTIONS

Two things are crucial when serving pops at parties: timing their entrance and remembering the napkins. Ten to fifteen minutes after they are removed from the freezer, they'll be too melted to serve. At cocktail parties, consider serving pops at intervals over the course of the evening.

Pops can be removed from the molds or served right in the molds so guests can remove the pops themselves. Cast the pops in individual pop molds, disposable paper molds, or nice glasses or plastic ware.

Serve pops directly on a plate, with or without a tray of ice. A grouping can be served on one large plate, or single pops can be served on individual dessert plates. They can also be served in an ice bucket filled with ice or in an ice cooler. This will keep them cool only for a short time, so they will need to be consumed quickly. Enclosing them in baggies or wrapping them in cellophane tied with a ribbon will keep them from sticking together.

Pops can accompany other foods and serve as appetizers or palette cleansers between courses. Serve pops on a bed of fresh fruit, on a wedge of melon, or on the side with a salad. Place one on a plate drizzled with chocolate, maple syrup, or strawberry sauce accompanied by a cookie, a piece of chocolate, or a handful of nuts.

TRANSPORTING ICE POPS

Unless you're driving a Good Humor truck, pops are tricky to take to a party. Your best bet is to prepare mini ice pops in small molds when you arrive. They will take a couple of hours to freeze and should be ready just in time for dessert. Ice cream pops are the easiest to make in the quickest amount of time. If you do want to bring pops from home, pack frozen pops in a cooler packed with ice or dry ice and put them in the host's freezer as soon as you arrive. Baggie pops (see page 122) are the easiest pops to transport.

Pop Tips

PERFECT PRESENTATION

- Prepare 2 or 3 mini pops or 1 large pop per person. Double this amount for cocktail parties.
- Make several types of pops to serve at one event.
- If you're short on time, prepare ice cream pops—they are quicker to make and freeze.
- Arrange pops in an attractive pattern on a tray of ice or serve in an ice bucket or cooler.
- Serve on top of a bed of fresh fruit or salad.
- Serve with accompaniments such as nuts, cookies, and chocolate.

Chapter 1

HEALTHY ENERGY POPS

After a rigorous workout, I find few things more satisfying than a healthy-delicious smoothie. Here's how to freeze these yummy energy drinks and enjoy them on a stick. Each *Healthy Energy Pop* is a study in contrasting flavors, the tastiest product of countless blending and freezing experiments. The ingredient combinations in these pops were created to take full advantage of seasonal fruits from local farmers' markets and to maximize the nutritional value of each pop. (The ingredients in *PB & Sesame Raspberry Pops* make up a complete protein!) Enriched with wheat germ, ginger, and flax and sunflower seeds, these pops provide an energy boost when you need it most.

Opposite: A selection of melon pops (clockwise from left): *Cantaloupe & Mint Pop, Watermelon & Almond Pop, Honeydew Melon Pop,* and striped melon pop (see page 34 for recipes, and see Layering, page 18, for how to make striped pops).

PB & SESAME RASPBERRY POPS

½ CUP PEANUT BUTTER

1 CUP PLAIN YOGURT

1 CUP MILK

4 TABLESPOONS HONEY

2 TEASPOONS PURE
VANILLA EXTRACT

1½ CUPS RASPBERRIES

2 CUPS RASPBERRY JUICE

4 TABLESPOONS
SESAME SEEDS

*Makes six 8-ounce pops
or eight 6-ounce pops*

This sophisticated pop is a surprisingly grown-up presentation of that much-loved peanut butter and jelly combination—and a powerful energy boost. The peanut butter is a good source of protein and monounsaturated fats, while the raspberries are rich in fiber, vitamins C and K, and manganese. Add the sesame seeds and you have a beautiful pop that's a complete protein, too.

1. Combine the peanut butter, yogurt, milk, 2 tablespoons of the honey, and the vanilla extract in a food processor or blender; process until smooth.
2. In a spouted cup, combine the raspberries and raspberry juice.
3. Partially fill the pop molds with the peanut butter mixture. Freeze for at least 1 hour.
4. Partially fill the molds with the raspberry mixture. Insert the sticks. Freeze for at least 1 hour.
5. Fill the molds with the remaining peanut butter mixture. Freeze for at least 8 hours.
6. Remove from the freezer; let stand at room temperature for 5 minutes before removing the pops from the molds.
7. Spoon some of the remaining honey around the rim of each pop. Sprinkle sesame seeds on the honey to coat. Enjoy peanut butter and jelly flavors in a whole new package!

ALT POPS!
Easy Blended Pops: Reduce the peanut butter to ⅓ cup, reduce the honey and sesame seeds to 2 tablespoons each, and omit the milk. Blend the peanut butter, yogurt, honey, vanilla extract, raspberries, and raspberry juice together until smooth, then stir in the sesame seeds. Pour into the pop molds. Insert the sticks and freeze for at least 6 hours.
PB & Banana Pops: Replace the raspberries with 3 overripe bananas and the raspberry juice with milk. Blend the banana and milk together.

NECTARINE CREAM POPS

1 CUP PEACH JUICE

3 ¾ CUPS CHOPPED NECTARINES

1 CUP MILK

1 CUP PLAIN YOGURT

2 TEASPOONS PURE VANILLA EXTRACT

2 TABLESPOONS WHEAT GERM

Makes six 8-ounce pops or eight 6-ounce pops

These pops and their peachy variation are luscious, sweet, and tangy. Like peaches, nectarines are a great source of fiber. They have more tang than peaches—and more vitamins A and C and potassium. Wheat germ, made from part of the wheat kernel, provides an additional nutritional boost: It is an antioxidant and one of the best sources of fiber and folic acid. Wheat germ combined with the milk and yogurt in this pop make a complete protein.

1. In a small bowl, combine the peach juice with ¾ cup of the nectarines. Set aside.
2. Combine 1 cup of the nectarines with the milk, yogurt, and vanilla extract in a food processor or blender; process until the mixture is smooth.
3. Stir in the remaining 2 cups nectarines and the wheat germ.
4. Partially fill the pop molds with the peach juice mixture and freeze for at least 2 hours. Fill the pop molds with the milk mixture. Insert the sticks. Freeze for at least 6 hours.
5. Remove from the freezer; let stand at room temperature for 5 minutes before removing the pops from the molds. Savor the nectarine's perfect balance of sweet and tangy.

ALT POPS!
Peach Cream Pops: Replace the nectarines with peaches.

Left: This pop was frozen in a repurposed juice box and uses a plastic spoon as the stick. To create the diagonal stripe, tilt the pop during freezing.

BANANA & DATE POPS

6 LARGE RIPE BANANAS, SLICED

1 CUP CHOPPED PITTED DATES

1 CUP MILK

1 CUP PLAIN YOGURT

2 TEASPOONS HONEY, HEATED FOR 30 SECONDS

1 TEASPOON PURE VANILLA EXTRACT

Makes six 8-ounce pops or eight 6-ounce pops

I first discovered this flavor combination while passing through a California desert in 118-degree heat. Like a mirage, a roadside stand appeared in the middle of nowhere selling banana date shakes. I knew immediately I had to incorporate this sweet and refreshing pairing into one of my pops. But this pop is more than a taste sensation: Both bananas and dates are good sources of carbohydrates, fiber, and potassium, and bananas provide us with many amino acids our bodies cannot produce.

1. Put the bananas, dates, milk, and yogurt in a food processor or blender; process until the mixture is smooth.
2. Add the honey and vanilla extract; process again to combine.
3. Fill the pop molds with the mixture. Insert the sticks. Freeze for at least 6 hours.
4. Remove from the freezer; let stand at room temperature for 5 minutes before removing the pops from the molds. Treat yourself to a delicious potassium fix.

ALT POPS!
Banana, Fig & Nut Pops: Replace the dates with 1 cup chopped dried figs or 2 cups chopped fresh figs. Stir 3/4 cup chopped hazelnuts into the banana-fig mixture.

STRAWBERRY & SUNFLOWER POPS

½ CUP HULLED
SUNFLOWER SEEDS

3 CUPS HULLED AND
HALVED STRAWBERRIES

¾ CUP STRAWBERRY
JUICE

¾ CUP PINEAPPLE JUICE

3 TABLESPOONS SUGAR

1 RIPE BANANA

3 TABLESPOONS LIGHT
CORN SYRUP

*Makes six 8-ounce pops
or eight 6-ounce pops*

If you can keep the birds from devouring the fruits and flowers in your garden, make these pops with homegrown strawberries and sunflower seeds. Strawberries and their juice are antioxidants high in vitamin C, manganese, and fiber, while sunflower seeds are a good source of vitamin E and believed to reduce cholesterol.

1. Preheat the oven to 300 degrees F. Put the sunflower seeds in a shallow pan and roast for 6 minutes, then stir and roast for 4 more minutes, or until lightly browned. Let cool.
2. In a saucepan, combine the strawberries, strawberry juice, pineapple juice, and sugar and simmer for 5 minutes over medium heat, stirring to dissolve the sugar. (If you like, push the mixture through a fine-mesh sieve and discard the strawberry seeds.)
3. Put the strawberry mixture in a food processor or blender and add the banana; process until smooth.
4. Stir in ⅓ cup of the sunflower seeds; reserve the rest.
5. Fill pop molds with the mixture. Insert the sticks. Freeze for at least 6 hours.
6. Remove from the freezer; let stand at room temperature for 5 minutes before removing the pops from the molds. Dip the edges of the pop in corn syrup and stick on the remaining seeds. Let this pop transport you to sunny summer days.

ALT POPS!
Creamy Strawberry & Banana Pops: Roasted sunflower seeds are optional. Process the strawberries and 2 bananas with ½ cup milk, ½ cup yogurt, and the sugar. Omit the pineapple juice.

Left: This *Strawberry & Sunflower Pop* was formed in a flower-shaped silicone baking mold (six flowers per mold).

BING CHERRY & VANILLA POPS

3 CUPS PITTED AND HALVED CHERRIES

1 CUP CHERRY JUICE

1 CUP PLAIN YOGURT

2 TEASPOONS PURE VANILLA EXTRACT

2 TEASPOONS HONEY

Makes six 8-ounce pops or eight 6-ounce pops

Cherry trees are not only gorgeous to look at, their fruits and juice pack a nutritional wallop. Rich in antioxidants, cherries also contain a cholesterol-lowering compound called beta-sitosterol. The only problem with them is that the season is way too short. Buy as many cherries as you can when they are available, pit them, and freeze them to extend your time with these pops.

1. Combine 2 cups of the cherries with the cherry juice, yogurt, vanilla extract, and honey in a food processor or blender; process until smooth.
2. Stir in the remaining 1 cup cherries.
3. Fill the pop molds with the mixture. Insert the sticks. Freeze for at least 6 hours.
4. Remove from the freezer; let stand at room temperature for 5 minutes before removing the pops from the molds. Take just one lick and you'll forget it's snowing.

ALT POPS!
Sour Cherry & Vanilla Pops: Before you begin step 1, simmer the cherry juice, ¼ cup sugar, and 3 cups sour cherries over low heat for 10 minutes. Let cool, then combine with the yogurt, vanilla extract, and honey and fill the pop molds with the mixture.

Left: To create this pop I separated the juice from the dairy, then added each to the mold in stages, tilting the mold during freezing to make the red racing stripe.

SUGAR PUMPKIN POPS

**2 1/2 CUPS PUMPKIN
PUREE, HOMEMADE OR
CANNED (SEE NOTES)**

1 CUP MILK

**1/2 CUP SWEETENED
CONDENSED MILK**

1 TEASPOON CINNAMON

**1/8 TEASPOON FRESHLY
GRATED NUTMEG**

**1 CUP ROASTED
HULLED PUMPKIN SEEDS
(SEE NOTES)**

*Makes six 8-ounce pops
or eight 6-ounce pops*

Native Americans treasured pumpkins for their dietary and medicinal properties. The orange color is from lutein, and alpha- and beta-carotene, nutrients that convert to vitamin A in the body and help to maintain eye health. Pumpkins are also rich in vitamin C. These pops are made with fresh sugar pumpkins. They are smaller and a darker orange than carving pumpkins and contain tasty seeds.

1. Combine the pumpkin puree, 1 1/2 cups water, 1/2 cup of the milk, 1/4 cup of the sweetened condensed milk, the cinnamon, and nutmeg in a food processor or blender; process until smooth. Stir in the pumpkin seeds.
2. In a bowl, combine the remaining 1/2 cup regular milk and 1/4 cup sweetened condensed milk.
3. Add the pumpkin mixture to the pop molds until about two thirds full. Freeze for at least 4 hours. Fill the molds to the top with the milk mixture and insert the sticks. Freeze for an additional 6 hours.
4. Remove from the freezer; let stand at room temperature for 5 minutes before removing the pops from the molds. Getting your dose of vitamin A and C has never been so much fun!

NOTES

When using canned pumpkin puree, add 1 additional cup of water.
To make homemade pumpkin puree: Cut a pumpkin in half and remove the seeds. (Reserve the seeds for roasting.) Bake at 375 degrees F for 1 1/2 hours. Let cool. Scoop the flesh from the skin into a food processor or blender and puree.
To roast the pumpkin seeds: Wash the seeds in a colander or sieve. Hull the seeds, spread them on a baking sheet, and bake for 15 minutes at 300 degrees F, or until browned.

Opposite: These pops were made in a silicone *cannelé* mold.

GINGER LEMON-LIME POPS

2 CUPS LEMONADE

1 CUP APPLE JUICE

½ CUP GINGER JUICE

¼ CUP FRESH LIME JUICE

4 TEASPOONS PEELED
AND GRATED FRESH
GINGER

2 TEASPOONS HONEY

1 LIME, PEELED AND CUT
INTO THIN ROUNDS

½ LEMON, PEELED AND
CUT INTO THIN ROUNDS

*Makes six 8-ounce pops
or eight 6-ounce pops*

Ginger's distinctive tang makes it an excellent palate cleanser. I recommend serving these pops between courses to prepare your guests for the exciting flavors to come. Ginger's health properties are also well known. For centuries, ginger extract has been used for its aphrodisiac powers, as a digestive aid, and as a pain reliever. So next time you have a tummy ache, treat yourself to this sweet comfort on a stick.

1. In a small saucepan, combine the lemonade, apple juice, ginger juice, lime juice, ginger, and honey. Put over low heat and simmer for 10 minutes.
2. Fill the pop molds with the lime and lemon slices. Add the juice mixture. Insert the sticks. Freeze for at least 6 hours.
3. Remove from the freezer; let stand at room temperature for 5 minutes before removing the pops from the molds. Take a lick of this tangy sweet treat.

ALT POPS!
Ginger & Coconut Pops: Replace the lemonade with 1½ cups coconut milk. Add 1½ cups chopped fresh coconut after step 1.

GREEN APPLE & FLAX SEED POPS

4 GRANNY SMITH APPLES, PEELED, CORED, AND DICED

2 CUPS PEAR JUICE

1/2 TEASPOON GROUND CARDAMOM

2 RIPE PEARS, PEELED, CORED, AND DICED

1 1/2 CUPS APPLESAUCE

3 TABLESPOONS FLAX SEED MEAL (GROUND FLAX SEEDS)

Makes six 8-ounce pops or eight 6-ounce pops

Pears provide a sweet counterpoint to the tartness of the Granny Smith apples in these pops. Feel free to enjoy them guilt-free, because new studies have found that apples may fight some types of cancers, help reduce cholesterol, and promote healthy lungs. The flax seed gives these pops an exotic nutty flavor. One of nature's most powerful cholesterol controllers, it is also rich in fiber, lignans (natural antioxidants), and omega-3 fats.

1. In a saucepan, combine the apples, pear juice, and cardamom. Simmer over low heat for 10 minutes, or until the apples are soft. Add the pears and simmer for 5 more minutes. Remove from the heat.
2. Stir in the applesauce and flax seed meal.
3. Fill the pop molds with the mixture. Insert the sticks. Freeze for at least 8 hours.
4. Remove from the freezer; let stand at room temperature for 5 minutes before removing the pops from the molds. Enjoy this antioxidant, fiber-rich snack on a stick!

ALT POPS!
Apple & Prickly Pear Cactus Pops: Use 2 apples. Replace the pears with 2 cups peeled, seeded prickly pear fruits. When available, use prickly pear juice instead of pear juice.
Maple, Pear & Flax Seed Pops: Replace the apples with pears. Add 1/4 cup maple syrup.

HONEYDEW MELON POPS

**4 CUPS DICED
(½-INCH CUBES) RIPE
HONEYDEW MELON**

⅓ CUP PLAIN YOGURT

JUICE OF 3 LIMES

GRATED ZEST OF 1 LIME

1 TABLESPOON HONEY

*Makes six 8-ounce pops
or eight 6-ounce pops*

Perfectly ripe honeydew melons are extraordinarily juicy and sweet. For these pops choose melons that are a little overripe, as they will have a high water content. (They'll be heavy for their size.) Honeydew is rich in vitamin C and potassium. Try layering the honeydew mixture with the watermelon and cantaloupe variations for beautiful pastel pops (see photo below, and see Layering, page 18, for further instructions).

1. Combine 2 cups of the melon with the yogurt, lime juice, and zest in a food processor or blender; process until smooth.
2. In a microwave-safe cup, heat the honey in a microwave oven for 30 seconds, until thinned.
3. Add the honey to the melon mixture; process again to combine.
4. Stir in the remaining 2 cups melon.
5. Fill the pop molds with the mixture. Insert the sticks. Freeze for at least 6 hours.
6. Remove from the freezer; let stand at room temperature for 5 minutes before removing the pops from the molds. Dip into this beautiful, amazingly juicy pop.

ALT POPS!

Watermelon & Almond Pops: Replace the honeydew melon with 5 cups diced watermelon, and replace the lime juice with 2 teaspoons almond extract. Stir in ⅓ cup sliced almonds after the watermelon mixture has been processed.

Cantaloupe & Mint Pops: Replace the honeydew melon with 4 cups diced cantaloupe, and replace the yogurt with ⅓ cup soy milk. Stir in 3 chopped fresh mint leaves after the melon mixture has been processed.

HALO-HALO
(PHILIPPINE SHAVED ICE TREATS)

1½ CUPS SHAVED ICE
(SEE NOTE)

2 TABLESPOONS
SWEETENED CONDENSED
MILK OR UNSWEETENED
COCONUT MILK

2 TABLESPOONS CUSTARD,
VANILLA PUDDING, OR
COOKED TAPIOCA PEARLS

2 TABLESPOONS FRUIT
SYRUP

2 TABLESPOONS SWEET
RED BEANS

1 TO 2 TABLESPOONS EACH
OF ANY COMBINATION
YOU LIKE:
sweet purple yam paste (ube);
cooked white beans, kidney
beans, or chickpeas; cooked
corn kernels; diced bananas
or plantains; palm seeds;
diced jackfruit, strawberry,
cantaloupe, honeydew melon,
papaya, mango, kiwi, star
apple, or avocado; shredded
coconut or coconut jelly

1 SCOOP ICE CREAM

PUFFED RICE CEREAL

Serves 1

Halo-halo means "mix-mix," and that's what this treat is about—mixing a delectable assortment of sweet and savory ingredients, including sweet beans and tapioca pearls, into shaved ice. Serve in a tall glass with a long spoon on a saucer (to catch the overflow). Or present the shaved ice and mix-ins at a party and invite your friends to create their own melt-in-your-mouth flavor combinations.

1. Pack the ice into a tall glass.
2. Pour in the sweetened condensed milk, custard, and fruit syrup; add the sweet red beans. The ingredients will sink into the ice. Mix-mix.
3. Add additional ingredients. Mix-mix.
4. Top with the ice cream and sprinkle with rice cereal. Serve at once.

NOTE
Hand-cranked and electric ice-shaving machines are available in most general merchandise stores in summertime and in Asian markets year round.

MORE ASIAN SHAVED ICE TREATS
Kakigori (Japan): Pack shaved ice into a bowl. Top with azuki bean paste, matcha (green tea powder), and sweetened condensed milk. Add a scoop of vanilla ice cream.
Bing Su (Korea): Pack shaved ice into a bowl. Top with sweet red beans, rice powder (available at Asian groceries), rice cakes, fruit, fruit syrup, and gummy candy.
Ice Kachang (Malaysia and Singapore): Put sweet red beans in a bowl with cooked rice noodles, cooked corn kernels, and coconut jelly. Top with shaved ice and palm sugar and fruit syrup.
Nam Kang Sai (Thailand): Put shaved ice in a bowl. Top with black sticky rice, coconut milk, taro paste, and nuts.

CARROT & WHEATGRASS POPS

3 ½ CUPS APPLE JUICE

½ CUP BROWN SUGAR

1 ½ CUPS PEELED AND DICED CARROTS

1 TEASPOON GROUND GINGER

½ TEASPOON CINNAMON

1 CUP COCONUT MILK, HOMEMADE (SEE PAGE 53) OR CANNED

1 CUP WHEATGRASS JUICE, FRESHLY SQUEEZED OR PREPARED FROM PREPACKAGED TABLETS

Makes six 8-ounce pops or eight 6-ounce pops

My love for growing grasses indoors inspired me to create wheatgrass pops. I wanted to combine the nutritious wheatgrass juice with something else, but I wasn't quite sure what. My apple juice and carrot breakthrough occurred when I spoke to my friends with kids, who revealed to me a whole world of pops specifically designed to disguise healthy vegetables.

1. In a saucepan, combine the apple juice and brown sugar and stir over low heat for 5 minutes to dissolve the sugar. Set aside 1½ cups of the mixture.
2. To the remaining apple juice mixture in the saucepan, add the carrots, ginger, and cinnamon. Bring to a boil over high heat, then lower the heat and simmer for 15 to 20 minutes, until the carrots are soft. Remove from the heat and pour into a bowl to cool to room temperature.
3. In a food processor or blender, puree the carrot mixture until smooth. Add ½ cup of the coconut milk and process to combine.
4. In a bowl, combine the wheatgrass juice, 3/4 cup of the reserved apple juice mixture, and the remaining ½ cup coconut milk.
5. Partially fill the ice pop molds with the carrot mixture. Insert the sticks. Freeze for at least 2 hours. Add a layer of the wheatgrass mixture, freeze for 2 hours, then add a layer of the remaining reserved apple juice mixture, and repeat, freezing for at least 2 hours between layers, until the pop molds are full. Freeze for at least 4 hours.
6. Remove from the freezer; let stand at room temperature for 5 minutes before removing the pops from the molds. Replace your daily wheatgrass shot with one of these pops.

ALT POPS!
Carrot, Orange & Wheatgrass Pops: Replace the apple juice with orange juice. Omit the coconut milk.
Carrot, Pineapple & Wheatgrass Pops: Replace the apple juice with pineapple juice. Add an additional 1 teaspoon ginger. Omit the cinnamon.

TROPICAL FRUIT POPS

2 CUPS CHOPPED GUAVA

1 CUP CHOPPED PAPAYA

1 ½ CUPS GUAVA NECTAR

2 TABLESPOONS HONEY

4 TABLESPOONS CREAM CHEESE

Makes six 8-ounce pops or eight 6-ounce pops

This pop was inspired by a visit to a bountiful market in Hilo, on the Big Island of Hawaii. The guava, one of my favorite fruits, contains five times more vitamin C than an orange and high amounts of calcium, unusual in a fruit. Papayas lend a sweet, musky taste to these pops, and serve up carbohydrates, vitamins A and C, calcium, iron, and fiber. The cream cheese in this pop celebrates the classic guava and cream cheese combo found in many tropical desserts.

1. Combine the guava, papaya, and guava nectar in a food processor or blender; process until smooth.
2. Add the honey and cream cheese; process again to combine until smooth.
3. Fill the pop molds with the mixture. Insert the sticks. Freeze for at least 6 hours.
4. Remove from the freezer; let stand at room temperature for 5 minutes before removing the pops from the molds. Take a bite out of this creamy, fruity pop—it's good for you!

ALT POPS!
Mango & Papaya Pops: Replace the guava with mango. Replace the cream cheese with 1 cup plain yogurt.

Left: This tube-shaped pop was formed in an empty paper towel roll; line the mold with waxed paper for easy removal after freezing.

WILD B BERRY POPS

1½ CUPS BLACKBERRIES

1½ CUPS BLUEBERRIES

1 CUP BLUEBERRY JUICE

1 CUP PLAIN YOGURT

2 TABLESPOONS HONEY

JUICE OF 1 LEMON

*Makes six 8-ounce pops
or eight 6-ounce pops*

If you're anything like me, taking a hike or bike ride during berry season is slow going, since it means stopping to pick and eat berries along the way. Then there's the question of what to do with the bushels of berries you bring home. *Wild B Berry Pops* are a fresh alternative to old standbys like berry cobbler. Better still, the blackberries contain vitamin A, antioxidants, and ellagic acid, which may help to prevent cancer, while the blueberries offer up vitamins C and E, and manganese. (See page 122 for a photo of these pops made in plastic baggie molds.)

1. Combine ¾ cup of the blackberries and ¾ cup of the blueberries with the blueberry juice, yogurt, honey, and lemon juice in a food processor or blender; process until smooth.
2. Stir in the remaining ¾ cup blackberries and the remaining ¾ cup blueberries.
3. Fill the pop molds with the mixture. Freeze for at least 6 hours.
4. Remove from the freezer; let stand at room temperature for 5 minutes before removing the pops from the molds. Berry delicious!

ALT POPS!

Red Berry Pops: Replace the blackberries and blueberries with 1 cup each cranberries, strawberries, and raspberries. Replace the blueberry juice with cranberry juice. Cook the cranberries in the cranberry juice over low heat for 10 minutes. Add more honey if necessary.

Chapter 2

FRUIT JUICE POPS

Short of pulling icicles off trees on cold winter days and eating them (and I am a big fan of that!), *Fruit Juice Pops* are the easiest and most popular frozen treats you can make. Simply pour the ingredients into ice pop molds and freeze. Through layering or mixing juices and fruit, you can create a myriad of flavor combinations. These pops are light enough to enjoy as a snack or between courses, and fancy enough to be served as an appetizer or dessert. Here you'll find classic flavor combinations and unexpected twists— from *Grape Pops* made with fresh grapes and home-squeezed juice, to refreshing *Apricot & Mint Pops*, to *Sour Plum Pops* featuring grilled salted plums embedded in plum ice.

Opposite: These globe-shaped pops (from top to bottom, *Pink & Yellow Grapefruit Pops, Honey Lemon-Lime Pops, and Tangerine & Blood Orange Pops*) were created in snap-together plastic Christmas ornaments. Simply drill a hole for the stick in one half, then fill and freeze each half separately. When the halves are frozen, snap the ornament together, use an eyedropper filled with juice to fill in any gaps in the pop, and freeze again.

TANGERINE & BLOOD ORANGE POPS

¼ CUP FRESH LEMON
JUICE

¼ CUP FRESH LIME JUICE

¼ CUP SUGAR

2½ CUPS FRESH
TANGERINE JUICE

2 CUPS FRESH BLOOD
ORANGE JUICE

3 TANGERINES, PEELED
AND DIVIDED INTO
SEGMENTS

*Makes six 8-ounce pops
or eight 6-ounce pops*

Living in southern California, with a tangerine and orange tree in the yard, I quickly came to appreciate the subtle differences among citrus fruits—and there was no going back to prepared juices! For parties I like to serve this citrus trio (as shown in photo on page 40, from top to bottom): *Pink & Yellow Grapefruit Pops, Honey Lemon-Lime Pops, and Tangerine & Blood Orange Pops.*

1. In a small bowl, combine the lemon and lime juices and the sugar, stirring to dissolve the sugar.
2. Stir in the tangerine juice and blood orange juice, then gently stir in the tangerine segments.
3. Fill the ice pop molds with the mixture. Insert the sticks. Freeze for at least 6 hours.
4. Remove from the freezer; let stand at room temperature for 5 minutes before removing the pops from the molds. Skip the orange juice tomorrow morning in favor of one of these pops!

ALT POPS!
Tangerine & Cranberry Pops: Replace the blood orange juice with cranberry juice. Add ¼ cup fresh or dried cranberries.
Orange Pops: Replace the tangerine juice and tangerine segments with orange juice and orange segments. Omit the blood orange juice.
Honey Lemon-Lime Pops: Replace the tangerine segments with 1 lime, peeled and cut into rounds. Increase the lemon juice to 1¾ cups and the lime juice to 1 cup. Replace the sugar with ¼ cup honey, and add 1¾ cups water and 2 drops of green food coloring in step 2.

PINK & YELLOW GRAPEFRUIT POPS

2 CUPS FRESH PINK GRAPEFRUIT JUICE

2 CUPS FRESH YELLOW GRAPEFRUIT JUICE

1 CUP SUGAR

½ PINK GRAPEFRUIT, PEELED AND SEPARATED INTO SEGMENTS

½ YELLOW GRAPEFRUIT, PEELED AND SEPARATED INTO SEGMENTS

6 OR 8 MARASCHINO CHERRIES (OPTIONAL)

Makes six 8-ounce pops or eight 6-ounce pops

These *Pink & Yellow Grapefruit Pops* have a sharp tang that really grows on you. Enjoy these pops alongside French toast or an omelet. To add a spark at lunch or dinner, serve them with a fresh salad.

1. Put the pink and yellow grapefruit juices into separate bowls and add ½ cup sugar to each. Stir until the sugar is dissolved. Stir the pink and yellow grapefruit segments into their respective bowls.

2. If you like, put a cherry in each pop mold. Partially fill the molds with the pink grapefruit juice mixture. Insert the sticks. Freeze for at least 2 hours. Add a layer of yellow grapefruit juice mixture, freeze for 2 hours, then add another layer of pink grapefruit; repeat, freezing for at least 2 hours between layers, until the pop molds are full. Freeze for at least 4 hours.

3. Remove from the freezer; let stand at room temperature for 5 minutes before removing the pops from the molds. Serve A.M., P.M., anytime.

ALT POPS!

Easy Blended Pops: In step 2, pour all the sweetened juices and segments together. Put a cherry in each pop mold. Pour the juice mixture into the molds. Insert the sticks and freeze for at least 8 hours.

Grapefruit & Strawberry Pops: Add ½ cup sliced strawberries to each of the juices in step 1.

Grapefruit Anise Pops: Simmer 4 whole star anise in ½ cup water for 20 minutes. Remove the anise. Add equal amounts of anise water to each of the juices in step 1.

Left: This pop was created in a twin-pop mold. To learn how to create the subtle pink and yellow bands, see Layering, page 18.

POMEGRANATE & APPLE POPS

8 WHOLE
POMEGRANATES,
OR 2 3/4 CUPS
POMEGRANATE JUICE

1/4 CUP FRESH LEMON
JUICE

1/2 CUP SUGAR

1 3/4 CUPS APPLE JUICE

3/4 CUP POMEGRANATE
SEEDS (FROM ABOUT
1/2 POMEGRANATE)

2 APPLES, CORED AND
SLICED (ROME APPLES
ARE BEST)

*Makes six 8-ounce pops
or eight 6-ounce pops*

When I first encountered a pomegranate, I was fascinated by its color, shape, taste, and the number of seeds (I counted almost six hundred!). Today, with evidence of the fruit's health benefits piling up, pomegranates are sold everywhere, especially in juice form. But if the health benefits aren't enough to compel you, the amazing flavor of these pops (not to mention the slyly embedded pomegranate seeds) should win you over.

1. If using whole pomegranates instead of juice, make several cuts in the pomegranate skin from top to bottom. Immerse a pomegranate in a bowl of water and gently break it apart. Pull the seeds away from the pith and they will sink. Strain off everything but the seeds. Drain the seeds in a colander. Repeat with the remaining pomegranates. Place the seeds in a food processor or blender, and blend until finely chopped. Strain through a fine-mesh sieve set over a large bowl. Stir in 1/8 cup of the lemon juice.
2. In a saucepan over low heat, simmer the sugar, apple juice, and the remaining 1/8 cup lemon juice until the sugar is dissolved. Let cool to room temperature.
3. Add half of the apple juice mixture to the pomegranate juice, along with the 3/4 cup seeds. Add the apples to the remaining apple juice mixture. Partially fill the molds with the pomegranate juice mixture. Insert the sticks. Freeze for at least 2 hours. Add a layer of the apple juice mixture, freeze for at least 2 hours, then add another layer of pomegranate; repeat, freezing for at least 2 hours between layers, until the pop molds are full. Freeze for at least 4 hours.
4. Remove from the freezer; let stand at room temperature for 5 minutes before removing the pops from the molds. Serve to health-conscious friends.

ALT POPS!
Easy Blended Pops: In step 3, pour all the juices together, add the seeds and apples, and pour into the pop molds. Insert the sticks and freeze for at least 8 hours.

GRAPE POPS

1 1/2 CUPS SEEDLESS RED GRAPES, CUT IN HALF

4 1/2 CUPS WHITE GRAPE JUICE, HOMEMADE (SEE NOTE) OR STORE-BOUGHT

Makes six 8-ounce pops or eight 6-ounce pops

I used to think there were two kinds of grapes—red and green. Upon further investigation I started noticing the many sizes and shapes and flavors. To date I have tasted seventeen different grapes, ranging from deeply fruity to super-sweet to tangy. Theoretically I could use one type of fresh grape and a different homemade fresh grape juice to come up with 289 variations of these *Grape Pops*. I recommend making just a few variations and serving them with cheese or at a finger-food party.

1. Divide the grape halves among the pop molds. Pour in the grape juice and insert the sticks. Freeze for at least 6 hours.
2. Remove from the freezer; let stand at room temperature for 5 minutes before removing the pops from the molds. Enjoy these pops as you would a fine wine.

NOTE

To make fresh grape juice: Wash 4 cups white grapes (about 6 pounds) and discard any that aren't firm. In batches, with a potato masher, mash the grapes so that all of them are popped. Put them in a large pot and add 2 cups water. Bring to a boil and cook over medium heat for 10 minutes, stirring and smashing the grapes occasionally. Remove from the heat and pour through a fine-mesh sieve or a colander lined with several layers of rinsed and squeezed cheesecloth. Add 1/2 cup sugar and stir until dissolved. Chill in the refrigerator for at least 10 minutes before using the juice for pops.

APRICOT POPS

½ CUP SUGAR

3 ½ CUPS BOTTLED
APRICOT NECTAR

2 CUPS FRESH APRICOTS,
HALVED AND PITTED

*Makes six 8-ounce pops
or eight 6-ounce pops*

There should be no debate that these beautiful orange pops strike a perfect balance between fruit and ice. The pure flavor of fresh apricots is enhanced when they are frozen into pops. To further enliven these pops, add fresh herbs and fruits in season. The apricot's short growing season makes these pops a rare treat.

1. In a saucepan, combine 1 cup water and the sugar. Stir continually over low heat until the sugar dissolves. Pour into a bowl and refrigerate for 10 minutes.
2. In a bowl, combine the apricot nectar and apricots. Stir in the sugar mixture.
3. Pour into the pop molds. Insert the sticks. Freeze for at least 8 hours.
4. Remove from the freezer; let stand at room temperature for 5 minutes before removing the pops from the molds. Serve with a simple slice of pound cake or a lemon cupcake.

ALT POPS!
Apricot & Basil or Mint Pops: Stir 2 tablespoons finely chopped fresh mint or basil into the nectar mixture in step 2.
Apricot & Cherry Pops: Reduce the apricots to ¾ cup. Stir 1½ cups fresh pitted cherries into the nectar mixture in step 2.

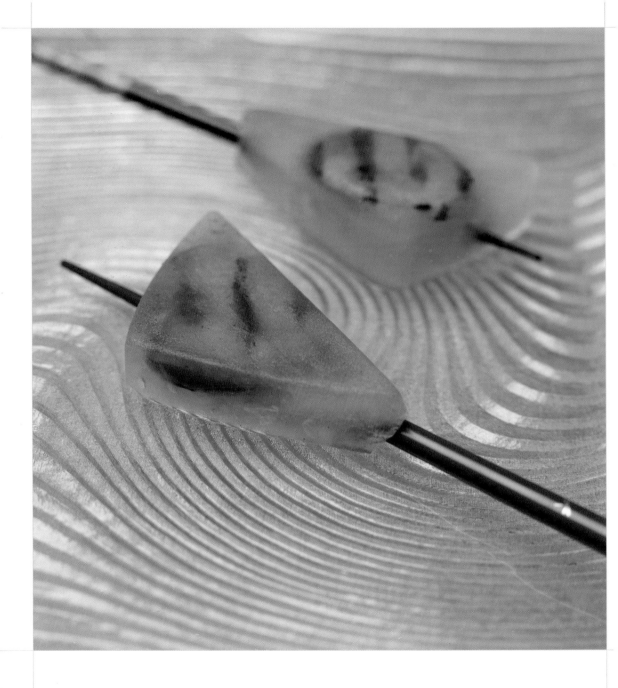

SOUR PLUM POPS

3 ½ CUPS SOUR PLUM
JUICE (SEE NOTE)

2 TABLESPOONS HONEY

JUICE OF 2 LIMES

2 CUPS RIPE SOUR PLUMS,
HALVED AND PITTED

COARSE SALT TO TASTE
(OPTIONAL)

*Makes six 8-ounce pops
or eight 6-ounce pops*

Sour plums (called *ume* in Japanese) are a common treat in Asia. This sweet and tangy fruit is used to make plum wine and in sweet and sour sauce. Sour plums are also sometimes grilled or smoked and sprinkled with salt, which is what inspired this unusual pops recipe.

1. In a small bowl, combine ½ cup of the sour plum juice with the honey and lime juice. Brush the mixture on both sides of the sour plums and sprinkle them with salt. Grill the plums or smoke them in a smoker until the plums are soft and slightly charred on both sides.
2. Put the grilled plums in the pop molds and pour in the remaining sour plum juice. Insert the sticks. Freeze for at least 8 hours.
3. Remove from the freezer; let stand at room temperature for 5 minutes before removing the pops from the molds. If you like salty sour plum, sprinkle some salt on each pop. These are real crowd pleasers at a barbecue.

NOTE
Sour plum juice and sour plums can be found at Asian grocery stores.

ALT POPS!
Sour Plum & Licorice Pops: Add 2 teaspoons licorice extract and 2 tablespoons chopped licorice leaves to the plum juice before pouring it into the molds in step 2.
Plum Pops: Replace the sour plum juice and plums with regular plum juice and plums. Omit the salt.

Opposite: These unique pops were created using custom silicone molds and chopsticks.

MULLED CIDER & WALNUT POPS

4½ CUPS FRESH
APPLE CIDER

1 CUP PACKED LIGHT
BROWN SUGAR

2 CINNAMON STICKS

½ TEASPOON GROUND
CARDAMOM

½ TEASPOON FRESHLY
GRATED NUTMEG

2 BAY LEAVES

6 WHOLE CLOVES

GRATED ZEST OF
1 ORANGE

1 APPLE, PEELED,
CORED, AND CUT INTO
THIN SLICES

½ CUP WALNUT HALVES

½ CUP GOLDEN RAISINS

*Makes six 8-ounce pops
or eight 6-ounce pops*

These pops are for those who, like me, can't resist stopping at roadside stands for mulled cider made from freshly pressed apples and spices. Tart and cloudy mulled cider is usually served hot, but it also tastes great frozen into pops. For spiked mulled cider pops, add 5 tablespoons rum or brandy to the cider mixture in step 2.

1. In a large pot, combine the cider, brown sugar, cinnamon sticks, cardamom, nutmeg, bay leaves, cloves, and orange zest. Bring to a boil over high heat, then lower the heat and simmer for 40 minutes. Pour the cider through a fine-mesh sieve set over a bowl and discard the solids.
2. Add the apple to the cider mixture. Put in the refrigerator for 1 hour to cool.
3. Roast the walnuts on a baking sheet for 5 minutes at 350 degrees F. Keep an eye on them to be sure they don't burn. Let cool.
4. Put the walnuts and golden raisins in the pop molds and pour in the cider. Insert the sticks. Freeze for at least 8 hours.
5. Remove from the freezer; let stand at room temperature for 5 minutes before removing the pops from the molds. See if this pop makes you dream of crisp, autumn days.

MANGO & CHILE *PALETAS*
(MEXICAN ICE POPS)

1 ¾ CUPS MANGO JUICE

⅓ CUP SUGAR

3 CUPS DICED MANGO

JUICE OF 2 LIMES

⅛ TEASPOON CHILE POWDER, OR TO TASTE

Makes six 8-ounce pops or eight 6-ounce pops

I was first introduced to *paletas* in San Miguel de Allende, Mexico. I was fascinated by the traditional flavors of these pops and tried them all, from *tejocate* (crabapple) and *nopales* (young prickly pear fruit) to corn and cream. Many of the *paleterias* throughout Mexico and the United States (where they're becoming more common) are operated by migrants from the Michoacan village of Tocumbo, where a three-story-high pop statue celebrates the global popularity of the local specialty. These pops strike a perfect balance of sweet, spicy, and cool.

1. In a saucepan, combine the mango juice and sugar; cook over low heat, stirring constantly, for about 5 minutes, until the sugar is dissolved. Set aside to cool.
2. In a food processor or blender, combine the diced mango and the lime juice; process until smooth. Pour in the mango juice mixture; process until smooth.
3. Gradually add the chile powder to taste, processing until combined.
4. Fill the pop molds with the mixture. Insert the sticks. Freeze for at least 6 hours.
5. Remove from the freezer; let stand at room temperature for 5 minutes before removing the pops from the molds. Serve with flair.

MORE MEXICAN *PALETAS*
Pineapple & Chile *Paletas*: Replace the mango with diced fresh pineapple and the mango juice with pineapple juice. Replace the lime juice with the juice of 1 lemon.
Cucumber & Jalapeño *Paletas*: Replace the mango with peeled, diced seeded cucumber. Replace the mango juice with plain yogurt and 1 teaspoon salt. Replace the chile powder with 1 small seeded minced fresh jalapeño (or more to taste). Note: Be sure to remove the membranes and seeds of the jalapeño, washing your hands thoroughly afterward.

CRANBERRY & RASPBERRY POPS

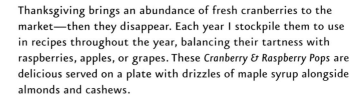

2 1/2 CUPS CRANBERRY JUICE

1 1/2 CUPS RASPBERRY JUICE

3/4 CUP FRESH CRANBERRIES

3/4 CUP RASPBERRIES

1 1/2 CUPS LIGHT BROWN SUGAR, OR TO TASTE

Makes six 8-ounce pops or eight 6-ounce pops

Thanksgiving brings an abundance of fresh cranberries to the market—then they disappear. Each year I stockpile them to use in recipes throughout the year, balancing their tartness with raspberries, apples, or grapes. These *Cranberry & Raspberry Pops* are delicious served on a plate with drizzles of maple syrup alongside almonds and cashews.

1. In a saucepan, combine all the ingredients and 2 cups water. Cook over low heat for about 7 minutes, stirring, until the mixture has thickened and the cranberries have popped open. Remove from the heat and let cool to room temperature.
2. Fill the pop molds with the mixture. Insert the sticks. Freeze for at least 12 hours.
3. Remove from the freezer; let stand at room temperature for 5 minutes before removing the pops from the molds. Serve to friends to show your thanks.

ALT POPS!

Cranberry & Apple or Grape Pops: Replace the raspberry juice and berries with apple juice and slices, or grape juice and grapes.

Cranberry & Almond or Cashew Pops: Omit the raspberry juice and raspberries. Use 4 cups cranberry juice. In step 1, after the cranberry mixture is removed from the heat, add 3/4 cup roasted almonds or roasted cashews.

Left: This heart-shaped *Cranberry & Raspberry Pop* was formed in a silicone baking mold. A red cocktail stirrer serves as the stick.

COCONUT POPS

1½ CUPS MILK

½ CUP SUGAR

1 TEASPOON PURE
VANILLA EXTRACT

3 CUPS COCONUT MILK,
HOMEMADE OR CANNED;
OR 3 CUPS COCONUT
WATER (SEE NOTE)

2 CUPS FRESH OR DRIED
SHREDDED COCONUT

*Makes six 8-ounce pops
or eight 6-ounce pops*

These Palm Beach–inspired pops are great on their own as a snack or paired with curry flavors. For rich and creamy pops, make them with fresh coconut milk; for light and refreshingly sweet pops, use fresh coconut water. Dried, shredded coconut can be added, but fresh is especially delicious.

1. In a saucepan, combine the milk and sugar and stir over low heat for 5 minutes to dissolve the sugar; be careful not to scald the milk. Stir in the vanilla extract and let cool to room temperature.
2. In a bowl, combine the coconut milk or coconut water, the shredded coconut, and the milk and vanilla mixture.
3. Pour into the pop molds. Insert the sticks. Freeze for at least 6 hours.
4. Remove from the freezer; let stand at room temperature for 5 minutes before removing the pops from the molds. Enjoy this coconut delight.

NOTE
To make homemade coconut milk: Put 2 cups grated coconut meat (from 1 coconut) and 3 cups hot water in a heatproof bowl. Let soak for 1 hour. Pour the coconut milk through a fine-mesh sieve set over a bowl.
To obtain coconut water: Coconut water is the liquid in the center of a fresh young (green) coconut. Drive 2 nails into the coconut, then remove them and drain the water out of the coconut into a bowl.

ALT POPS!
Coconut & Banana Pops: Replace 1 cup of the coconut with 1½ cups mashed ripe bananas. Add the mashed bananas in step 2.
Coconut Curry Pops: Omit the vanilla extract. Gradually add red, green, or yellow curry paste to taste plus 2 tablespoons chopped fresh mint leaves and 3 tablespoons fresh lime juice in step 2.

KIWI POPS

1 1/2 CUPS SUGAR

3 CUPS SLICED KIWIS, WITH OR WITHOUT THE PEEL

3/4 CUP FRESH LIME JUICE

Makes six 8-ounce pops or eight 6-ounce pops

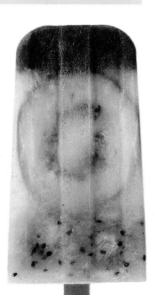

To me, kiwis taste like a combination of strawberry, banana, and pineapple. In many recipes they are combined with these fruits, but I also like to experience the subtle taste of kiwi on its own—tweaking the taste buds by serving them alongside a plate of fresh strawberries and pineapple.

1. In a saucepan, combine 1 cup water and the sugar. Stir over low heat until the sugar dissolves. Refrigerate for 10 minutes to cool.
2. Combine the kiwis and the lime juice in a food processor or blender. Process until smooth.
3. Add the sugar water and 1 1/2 cups cold water to the kiwi mixture and process again to combine.
4. Pour the mixture into the pop molds. Insert the sticks. Freeze for at least 6 hours.
5. Remove from the freezer; let stand at room temperature for 5 minutes before removing the pops from the molds. Get ready to tweak your taste buds!

ALT POPS!
Kiwi & Strawberry Pops: Reduce the kiwi to 2 cups. Add 1 cup strawberries in step 2. Add an additional 1/2 cup sliced strawberries to the molds in step 4.
Kiwi & Pineapple Pops: Reduce the kiwi to 2 cups. Replace the water with pineapple juice. Add 1 1/2 cups fresh pineapple chunks to the molds in step 4.

Left: For this *Kiwi & Strawberry Pop*, the kiwis and strawberries were pureed separately, and kiwi slices were added to the lime juice. The sugar water was divided among the three mixtures, which were then frozen in layers. Opposite: These petite *Kiwi*, *Apricot*, and *Coconut Pops* were made in pyramid-shaped candy molds. (For recipes, see above and pages 47 and 53.)

Chapter 3

SODA FOUNTAIN POPS

Stopping at soda fountain counters is one of my favorite things to do on a road trip. In big cities, the soda fountain is nearly obsolete except for a few nostalgic holdouts, but in small towns it still serves as a meeting place for people of all ages, where frothy root beer floats, sweet strawberry sodas, and extravagantly dressed banana splits mingle at the counter with high-school gossip and local politics. These *Soda Fountain Pops* are based on tasty discoveries I've enjoyed on the open road. Keep your eyes open for regional soda fountain specialties when you're out and about—chances are, they'd make great pops too.

Opposite: This *Banana Split Pop* was formed in a plastic cup. If the ice cream is frozen solid, the cup will slip right off. If it's a little soft, use scissors to carefully cut off the cup. (See page 70 for the recipe.)

ROOT BEER FLOAT POPS

4 CUPS ROOT BEER

6 OR 8 MARASCHINO CHERRIES, STEMMED

2 ½ CUPS VANILLA ICE CREAM

Makes six 8-ounce pops or eight 6-ounce pops

This frothy, spicy pop is inspired by my teenage precoffee addiction to root beer floats. Tiny bubbles in the ice cream trigger the formation of large bubbles of carbon dioxide when combined with root beer. To make these pops solid, you have to cut down on the characteristic foam a bit by carefully lowering the ice cream into the root beer and scooping any foam that does form off the top.

1. Pour cold root beer into a pitcher and put it in the freezer for 10 minutes. (This will make it very cold and reduce the ice cream melt factor.)
2. Put a cherry in each mold. Pour some root beer into each mold until it is half full.
3. Gently lower a small scoop of ice cream into each pop mold so it is about three quarters full.
4. Slowly add more root beer until the molds are full. Scoop off the foam with a spoon. Freeze for at least 6 hours.
5. Remove from the freezer; let stand at room temperature for 5 minutes before removing the pops from the molds. It's time for a nostalgic treat!

Opposite: To create the diagonal stripe, tilt the pop during freezing so one corner is lower than the rest of the pop. The root beer and cherries will slide to that corner, creating a colorful stripe.

ALT POPS!

Black Cow Float Pops: Before chilling the root beer in step 1, stir in $^1/_2$ cup chocolate syrup.

Egg Cream Float Pops: Replace the root beer with $2^1/_2$ cups seltzer and $^1/_3$ cup chocolate syrup. When you add the ice cream in step 3, pour in $1^1/_2$ cups milk along with it.

Birch Beer Float Pops: Replace the root beer with birch beer and $^1/_2$ cup chocolate syrup.

Boston Cooler Float Pops: Replace the root beer with ginger ale.

Cream Cooler Float Pops: Replace the root beer with cream soda.

Sarsaparilla Float Pops: Replace the root beer with sarsaparilla soda.

Passion Fruit Float Pops: Replace the root beer with $2^1/_2$ cups lemon-lime soda and 2 cups passion fruit juice and add the juice of 1 lemon and 1 lime. Omit the maraschino cherries. Replace the ice cream with lemon or lime sherbet.

Tropical Fruit Float Pops: Make the passion fruit variation above, substituting guava nectar or papaya juice for the passion fruit juice.

STRAWBERRY SODA POPS

6 OR 8 STRAWBERRIES

**1 CUP CHOPPED
BITTERSWEET CHOCOLATE**

**4 CUPS STRAWBERRY
SODA**

*Makes six 8-ounce pops
or eight 6-ounce pops*

These brightly colored, fruity pops are the perfect way to
indulge in the over-the-top sweet flavors kids love. A trip to
the Strawberry Festival in Ventura, California, provided the
inspiration. Thirsty after eating too many chocolate-covered
strawberries, I grabbed a strawberry soda, and the idea for
this fizzy pop was born.

1. Choose small strawberries that will fit into your pop molds. If necessary, cut
   them in half to fit. Stick a strawberry onto the end of each pop stick.
2. Heat the chocolate in the top of a double boiler over medium-low heat
   (simmering water in the double boiler), being careful not to let any
   water get in the chocolate or it may become grainy. Stir constantly
   until the chocolate is almost melted. Remove from the heat and stir
   until smooth. Dip the strawberries into the melted chocolate one at a
   time. Lay them on a foil-covered tray. Put them in the freezer for at
   least 1 hour.
3. Fill the molds with cold strawberry soda. Put the mold in the freezer
   for about 20 minutes, until it is very cold but not yet frozen.
4. Insert the chocolate strawberries into the soda. Freeze for at least 6 hours.
5. Remove from the freezer; let stand at room temperature for 5 minutes
   before removing the pops from the molds. These pops instantly
   sweeten up summer.

ALT POPS!
Grape Soda Pops: Stick a few grapes onto the sticks instead of strawberries. Omit the chocolate. Replace the strawberry soda with grape soda.
Orange Soda Pops: Stick a peeled orange slice onto each stick instead
of the strawberry. Omit the chocolate. Replace the strawberry soda
with orange soda. (If you like, you can add a small scoop of vanilla ice
cream; lower it carefully into the partially frozen soda before you insert
the orange slice.)

CHERRY COLA POPS

4 CUPS COLA

1 CUP BOTTLED SOUR CHERRY JUICE

¼ CUP CHERRY ITALIAN SYRUP (AVAILABLE AT GOURMET STORES), OR 6 TABLESPOONS CHERRY EXTRACT

¼ CUP PITTED SOUR CHERRIES

Makes six 8-ounce pops or eight 6-ounce pops

In their heyday in the 1950s, soda fountains were equipped with a huge selection of flavorings that highly skilled soda jerks would add to colas. Today the most unusual flavors live on only in memory, but cherry cola is an enduring survivor. These pops will take you back to a time when even soda could be made to order.

1. Combine the cola, cherry juice, and Italian syrup in a pitcher. Let sit for about 5 minutes, until the fizz dissipates.
2. Divide the cherries evenly among the pop molds. Pour the cola mixture into the molds. Insert the sticks. Freeze for at least 6 hours.
3. Remove from the freezer; let stand at room temperature for 5 minutes before removing the pops from the molds. Serve with a flourish. (It's all in the wrist, as any good soda jerk will tell you.)

ALT POPS!
Vanilla Cola Pops: Use $4^2/3$ cups cola. Replace the cherry juice and syrup with 3 teaspoons pure vanilla extract and ¼ cup vanilla Italian syrup. Omit the sour cherries.
Lemon-Lime Cola Pops: Replace the cola with lemon-lime soda and the cherry juice and syrup with the juice of 2 lemons and 3 limes, 1 teaspoon grated lemon zest, and 1 teaspoon grated lime zest. Omit the sour cherries.
Italian Soda Pops: Use any flavor of Italian syrup and replace the cola with 3 cups carbonated water and 1 cup milk. Omit the sour cherries.

Opposite: This gem-shaped *Strawberry Soda Pop* was made in a silicone ice cube mold shaped like a precious jewel. A decorative cocktail pick serves as the stick.

BUBBLY FRUIT JUICE POPS

4 CUPS CARBONATED FRUIT JUICE, OR 2 CUPS JUICE AND 2 CUPS SPARKLING WATER

1 CUP FRESH FRUIT OF THE SAME TYPE AS THE JUICE

Makes six 8-ounce pops or eight 6-ounce pops

I like to collect bottles and cans of local beverages from gas stations across the country, trying different pops with these colorful sodas and recycling the odd-shaped plastic bottles as pop molds. These *Bubbly Fruit Juice Pops* are a cool way to satisfy your thirst and replenish your energy all at once, and the variations are endless: Just select your favorite carbonated beverage.

1. Put the carbonated fruit juice in a pitcher. Let sit for about 5 minutes, until the fizz dissipates.

2. Divide the fruit evenly among the pop molds. Pour the juice mixture into the molds. Freeze for at least 6 hours.

3. Remove from the freezer; let stand at room temperature for 5 minutes before removing the pops from the molds. These fizzy pops will put a bounce in your step.

ALT POPS!
Thirst Quencher Soda Pops: Replace the carbonated fruit juice with half electrolyte balance drink and half club soda.
Energy Soda Pop: Replace the carbonated fruit juice with half super-caffeinated energy drink and half fruit juice, and add 1 cup club soda. Omit the fruit.
Ginseng Cola or Ginger Beer Pops: Replace the carbonated fruit juice with sparkling ginseng cola or ginger beer.

YOGURT 50/50 POPS

2 CUPS ORANGE SHERBERT

⅓ CUP FRESH ORANGE JUICE

2 CUPS VANILLA YOGURT

⅓ CUP MILK

Makes six 8-ounce pops or eight 6-ounce pops

These frosty orange and vanilla pops incorporate the flavors that made Creamsicles famous, but the yogurt makes them lower in fat than those iconic pops. Try pairing the yogurt with raspberry or lime sherbert. I follow tradition with these pops and hide the yogurt in the center, but the flavor combination will be familiar whether they are blended, marbleized, or layered. For best results use silicone molds, paper cups, or push-up molds (as shown in the photo below).

1. In a bowl, combine the sherbert with the orange juice. Create a shell of the sherbert mixture by pressing it around the inside edges of the pop molds. Put in the freezer for 2 hours to harden.
2. In a bowl, combine the yogurt and milk.
3. With a pastry bag, squeeze the yogurt mixture into the center of the sherbert shell. Insert the sticks. Freeze for at least 8 hours.
4. Remove from the freezer. Serve these popular pops immediately after they are removed from the mold.

NOTE

Push-up molds, silicone molds, or paper cups are the best molds to use for these pops (and any other pop that includes ice cream, sherbert, or frozen yogurt), as they will soften quickly, making them difficult to remove from upright molds.

ALT POPS!

Raspberry 50/50 Pops: Replace the orange sherbert with raspberry sherbert and the orange juice with raspberry juice.
Lime 50/50 Pops: Replace the orange sherbert with lime sherbert and the orange juice with lime juice.

MINT CHOCOLATE POPS

1 (1.75-QUART) BOX
MINT CHOCOLATE CHIP
ICE CREAM

12 OR 16 MINT WAFER
CANDIES (2 PER POP)

*Makes six 8-ounce pops
or eight 6-ounce pops*

These deliciously simple mint chocolate pops are made from mint ice cream sandwiched between two mint wafer candies. They have a super-cool melt-in-your-mouth sweetness reminiscent of everyone's favorite Girl Scout cookie.

1. Fold down one long side of the ice cream container and use a large knife to cut the ice cream into squares the size of the candies.
2. Lay a candy on a work surface, face down, and top with a square of ice cream. Cover with another candy, face up. Press the sandwich together gently. Insert the sticks in the ice cream. Freeze for 1 hour to harden. Enjoy these minty fresh pops.

ALT POPS!
Peanut & Chocolate Pops: Replace mint candies with squares of your favorite chocolate bar. Spread peanut butter on the bottom sides of the chocolate squares before making the sandwich. Replace the mint ice cream with chocolate ice cream.
Chocolate & Raisin Pops: Replace the mint candies with squares of your favorite chocolate bar. Replace the mint ice cream with chocolate ice cream. Press chocolate-covered raisins into the ice cream.

COOKIE DOUGH POPS

2 ½ CUPS ALL-PURPOSE FLOUR

1 TEASPOON BAKING SODA

1 TEASPOON SALT

1 CUP UNSALTED BUTTER

¾ CUP GRANULATED SUGAR

¾ CUP BROWN SUGAR

1 TEASPOON PURE VANILLA EXTRACT

2 CUPS CHOCOLATE CHIPS

1 CUP WALNUTS, CHOPPED

2 LARGE EGGS

4 CUPS VANILLA ICE CREAM (OR YOUR FAVORITE FLAVOR)

Makes six 8-ounce pops or eight 6-ounce pops

This half-baked recipe is for anyone who loves ice cream sandwiches but would prefer to eat them in our favorite form—on a stick. Using the ice cream mix-in method (see page 13 for ideas), you can prepare your own favorite ice creams and sandwich them between any kind of cookie you can think of—or even waffles! Waffles and ice cream was the only ice cream concoction my mom would allow me to eat for breakfast.

1. Preheat the oven to 375 degrees F. Lightly grease 2 large baking sheets.
2. In a bowl, combine the flour, baking soda, and salt. Set aside.
3. In a separate bowl, beat the butter, sugars, vanilla extract, and ½ cup water together until creamy. Fold into the flour mixture until completely combined.
4. Stir in the chocolate chips and walnuts.
5. Set aside one third of the dough. Add the eggs to the remaining two thirds dough. Mix with a wooden spoon or an electric mixer until thoroughly incorporated.
6. Drop the egg dough in 1-tablespoon balls onto the baking sheets. Bake for 10 to 12 minutes, until golden. Let cool and remove from the baking sheets with a spatula.
7. Break the reserved dough into 1-teaspoon pieces and stir them into the ice cream. Freeze for 10 minutes.
8. Assemble the pops: Put 1 scoop of the ice cream on the bottom side of one of the cookies, spreading the ice cream evenly with a spatula. Cover with another cookie. Press together gently.
9. Insert sticks into the ice cream. Serve immediately or, if you can wait, put in an airtight container and freeze for 1 hour.

ALT POPS!

Waffles & Ice Cream Pops: Use waffles cut to pop size to sandwich your favorite ice cream loaded with your favorite mix-ins.

Peanut Butter Cookie Pops: Use peanut butter cookies, and mix peanut butter into chocolate ice cream.

Ginger Snap Pops: Use ginger snap cookies (store-bought or homemade), and mix crushed ginger snaps into vanilla ice cream.

S'Mores Ice Cream Pops: Use chocolate-covered graham crackers, and mix mini marshmallows into chocolate ice cream.

Cookies & Cream Pops: Separate sandwich cookies into two halves. Place a small scoop of ice cream on one cookie and press the other cookie on top. Insert the stick into the ice cream.

CHOCOLATE-DIPPED POPS

4 CUPS VANILLA OR
CHOCOLATE ICE CREAM

2 CUPS CHOPPED
CHOCOLATE
(WHITE, MILK, DARK,
OR BITTERSWEET)

1/2 CUP TOPPING,
SUCH AS CHOPPED NUTS,
SPRINKLES, TOFFEE BITS,
OR SHREDDED COCONUT

*Makes six 8-ounce pops
or eight 6-ounce pops*

Biting into an ice cream pop coated with a thick chocolate shell is a creamy and delicious experience. Topping the chocolate with nuts, coconut, sprinkles, or toffee is pure decadence. Try different chocolates for different tastes.

1. For round pops, pack the ice cream into 1-inch deep round paper cups. For square or rectangular pops, cut the ice cream from a rectangular container into pop-sized pieces. Insert the sticks. Freeze for 1 hour to harden.
2. While the pops are in the freezer, heat the chocolate in the top of a double boiler over medium-low heat (simmering water in the double boiler). Stir constantly until the chocolate is almost melted. Remove from the heat and stir until smooth. Let cool to room temperature but do not let it sit until hardened.
3. Remove 1 pop from the mold. Dip the pop into the chocolate, turning it until covered. Let the excess chocolate drip onto a plate. Sprinkle the topping over the chocolate, pressing lightly with the flat edge of a knife to help it adhere. Repeat with the remaining pops. Serve immediately, or prop the sticks in a piece of Styrofoam, cover with plastic baggies, and store in the freezer until ready to serve.

Opposite: Mix and match chocolate varieties and toppings, as shown (from left to right): white chocolate and almonds, milk chocolate and walnuts, bittersweet chocolate and coconut, and a simple dark chocolate–dipped pop.

BANANA SPLIT POPS

1/3 CUP STRAWBERRY
TOPPING

1/2 RIPE BUT FIRM
BANANA (CUT
CROSSWISE) FOR
EACH POP

1 1/2 CUPS STRAWBERRY
ICE CREAM

1/3 CUP PINEAPPLE
TOPPING

1 1/2 CUPS VANILLA
ICE CREAM

1/3 CUP CHOCOLATE
FUDGE

1 1/2 CUPS CHOCOLATE
ICE CREAM

WHIPPED CREAM

1/4 CUP CHOPPED
WALNUTS

6 OR 8 MARASCHINO
CHERRIES

*Makes six 8-ounce pops
or eight 6-ounce pops*

This king of pops is based on the classic flavors of a banana split, and they're all here—pineapple and strawberry toppings included. I put the banana on the pop stick to create a hidden surprise. (See the photo on page 56.)

1. Use paper cups as molds for these pops (see page 118). Divide the strawberry topping among the paper cup molds. Stick the banana halves onto the pop sticks and place in the molds. Freeze for 1 hour.
2. Top with the strawberry ice cream and the pineapple topping, packing the ice cream and topping around the bananas to hide them. Freeze for 1 hour.
3. Top with the vanilla ice cream and the chocolate fudge. Add the chocolate ice cream. Freeze for 6 hours.
4. Peel off and discard the paper cups. Top each pop with whipped cream, walnuts, and a cherry. Enjoy your banana split on a stick!

ALT POPS!
Neopolitan Malt Pops: Omit the strawberry, pineapple, and chocolate fudge toppings. Let the ice creams soften in separate bowls, then stir 1 tablespoon malt powder and 1/2 cup malt balls into each. Freeze the bowls for 20 minutes, then pack the ice creams in layers into paper cup molds. Insert the sticks and freeze for at least 3 hours. Peel off the cups and garnish the top of each pop with a malt ball. Omit the banana, whipped cream, walnuts, and cherries.
Italian Spumoni Pops: Make the *Neopolitan Malt Pops* variation above, omitting the malt powder and malt balls and replacing the strawberry and vanilla ice creams with cherry and pistachio.

CREMOLATAS
(ITALIAN WATER ICES)

1 CUP SLICED ALMONDS

1 1/4 CUPS PACKED LIGHT BROWN SUGAR

1 1/2 CUPS WHOLE MILK

1 1/2 CUPS HEAVY CREAM

2 TEASPOONS ALMOND EXTRACT

Serves 6

Italians are prolific creators of icy treats—they can lay claim to granita, sorbet, gelato, and (my favorite) *cremolata*, or Italian water ice. It has a light texture and can be prepared in creamy or fruity versions. To make *cremolata*, a flavored mixture is frozen and then shaved to serve. Many of the pop recipes in this book can be made into water ices: Freeze the pop mixture in an ice cube tray and process the cubes in an ice shaver as described below.

1. Preheat the oven to 300 degrees F. Spread the almonds on a baking sheet and sprinkle with 6 tablespoons water and 1/4 cup of the brown sugar. Toast in the oven for 3 minutes. Remove from the oven and grind in a food processor or blender until fine.
2. In a saucepan, bring the milk to a boil over low heat, then remove from the heat. Add the remaining 1 cup brown sugar and stir until dissolved. Stir in the cream and almond extract.
3. Freeze in ice cube trays for 3 to 4 hours, until hard. Process cubes in an ice shaver or food processor or blender until the cubes are broken up but not slushy. Serve in the traditional pleated white paper cups.

NOTE
Hand-cranked and electric ice-shaving machines are available in most general merchandise stores in summertime and in Asian markets year round.

MORE WATER ICES
Chocolate Water Ice: In a saucepan, bring 4 cups water and 2 cups granulated sugar to a boil, stirring until the sugar is dissolved. Stir in 1 1/4 cups Dutch-process cocoa powder and 1/4 teaspoon cinnamon and proceed with step 4.
Limoncello Water Ice: In a saucepan, bring 4 cups water and 2 cups granulated sugar to a boil, stirring until the sugar is dissolved. Stir in 3/4 cup fresh lemon juice and the zest of 1 lemon and proceed with step 4.

Chapter 4

CREAM &
PUDDING
POPS

Shamelessly rich and irresistibly comforting, *Cream & Pudding Pops* are sure to please.
I love their firm, satiny texture, which can easily be dressed up with mix-ins—think
nuts, raisins, tapioca, fruit, and chocolate chips—because the thickness of the pudding,
mascarpone cheese, eggnog, or custard helps suspend the mix-ins evenly throughout the
pop. (An added bonus of cream- and pudding-based pops is that they rarely drip as you're
eating them.) You can use prepared pudding for these pops with good results, but it's so
much more fun if you make your own.

Opposite: This *Blueberry Cheesecake Pop* and the *Strawberry and
Chocolate Cheesecake Pop* variations were made in square silicone
molds. (See page 74 for recipes.)

BLUEBERRY CHEESECAKE POPS

BLUEBERRY TOPPING

3/4 CUP BLUEBERRIES

1 1/2 TABLESPOONS CORNSTARCH, SIFTED

2 TEASPOONS FRESH LEMON JUICE

1/4 CUP SUGAR

CHEESECAKE

8 OUNCES CREAM CHEESE

1/2 CUP SUGAR

1/2 CUP SOUR CREAM

1 CUP HEAVY CREAM

2 TEASPOONS PURE VANILLA EXTRACT

2 CUPS BLUEBERRIES

CRUST

10 GRAHAM CRACKERS

6 TABLESPOONS SUGAR

4 TABLESPOONS UNSALTED BUTTER, MELTED

Makes six 8-ounce pops or eight 6-ounce pops

These pops are based on my all-time favorite rendition of my classic no-bake cheesecake recipe. Silicone molds or paper cups are the best molds for these pops. (See page 72 for photo.)

1. To make the topping: In a saucepan, combine the blueberries, 3/4 cup water, the cornstarch, lemon juice, and sugar and cook over low heat, stirring, for 5 minutes. Remove from the heat and let the topping stand to thicken. Set aside.

2. To make the cheesecake: In a bowl, beat the cream cheese, sugar, and sour cream together until blended.

3. In a separate bowl, whip the cream and vanilla extract until the cream just starts to thicken, 1 to 2 minutes. Add to the cream cheese mixture and beat for 30 seconds. Gently stir in the blueberries. Set aside.

4. To make the crust: In a food processor or blender, grind the graham crackers into crumbs. Add the sugar and process until combined. Transfer to a bowl and add the butter and 3 tablespoons water, stirring until sticky. Refrigerate until needed.

5. Pour the topping into each mold until it is one quarter full. Freeze for 2 hours.

6. Pour the cheesecake mixture into each mold, leaving 1/2 inch at the top of each mold for the crust. Insert the stick. Freeze for 3 hours.

7. Press the crust into the pop molds. If the crust is not sticking together, add more water. Freeze for at least 4 hours.

8. Remove from the freezer; let stand at room temperature for 5 minutes before removing the pops from the molds.

ALT POPS!
Strawberry Cheesecake Pops: Replace the blueberries with sliced strawberries.
Chocolate Cheesecake Pops: Replace the graham crackers with chocolate cookies and shaved chocolate. Replace the blueberries with chocolate chips and 1/2 cup chocolate fudge sauce.

PERSIMMON PUDDING POPS

3/4 CUP BROWN SUGAR

1/2 TEASPOON CINNAMON

1/4 TEASPOON GROUND GINGER

3/4 CUP CORNSTARCH

1/4 TEASPOON SALT

3 1/2 CUPS MILK

4 TABLESPOONS UNSALTED BUTTER

3/4 CUP PUREED SOFT PERSIMMONS

2 TEASPOONS PURE VANILLA EXTRACT

3/4 CUP CHOPPED SOFT PERSIMMONS

Makes six 8-ounce pops or eight 6-ounce pops

Hardy persimmon and cold-loving quince are two fruits that can withstand a deep freeze. One especially cold year, I was inspired to rethink the warm desserts usually associated with these fruits and turn them into icy treats.

1. In a saucepan, stir together the brown sugar, cinnamon, ginger, cornstarch, and salt.
2. Add the milk and bring to a boil over medium heat, stirring constantly. Remove from the heat as soon as the mixture begins to thicken.
3. Stir in the butter until melted and combined. Add the pureed persimmons and the vanilla extract. Refrigerate for 20 minutes.
4. Stir in the chopped persimmons.
5. Pour into the pop molds. Insert sticks. Freeze for at least 8 hours.
6. Remove from the freezer; let stand at room temperature for 5 minutes before removing the pops from the molds. Serve on a crisp fall day when the leaves are the color of your pops.

ALT POPS!
Maple & Quince Pudding Pops: Simmer 2 large quinces in 2 1/2 cups water until soft (about 40 minutes). Peel, then puree enough to yield 3/4 cup puree. Replace the brown sugar with 1/2 cup maple syrup. Replace the chopped persimmon with 1/4 cup chopped walnuts.
Persimmon, Ice Cream & Applesauce Pops: Ice cream and applesauce are often paired with persimmons, and make for pretty layered pops. Pour some of the persimmon mixture into the pops, freeze for 2 hours, then add a layer of ice cream and freeze again; fill the molds with applesauce and freeze again.

EGGNOG POPS

Holidays wouldn't be the same without eggnog. But there's no reason you can't have a little fun with tradition. Transform this creamy brew into tasty, spicy ice pops. Joy and merriment will be had by all! If you want to make spiked *Eggnog Pops*, replace the rum extract with 5 tablespoons rum.

6 TABLESPOONS VANILLA CUSTARD POWDER

4 CUPS EGGNOG (SEE NOTE)

1/2 CUP SUGAR

3 TEASPOONS RUM EXTRACT

2 TEASPOONS PURE VANILLA EXTRACT

1/2 TEASPOON FRESHLY GRATED NUTMEG

1/2 TEASPOON CINNAMON, PLUS A FEW PINCHES FOR SPRINKLING

3/4 CUP HEAVY CREAM

Makes six 8-ounce pops or eight 6-ounce pops

1. In a saucepan, combine the custard powder, eggnog, and sugar and stir over medium-low heat until the powder and sugar are dissolved. Pour into a bowl or pitcher.
2. Whisk in the rum and vanilla extracts, nutmeg, and the 1/2 teaspoon cinnamon.
3. Whip the cream until it just starts to thicken, 1 to 2 minutes. Fold the cream into the eggnog mixture to create a marbled pattern.
4. Pour into the pop molds. Insert the sticks. Freeze for at least 8 hours.
5. Remove from the freezer; let stand at room temperature for 5 minutes before removing the pops from the molds. Sprinkle some additional cinnamon on each pop. Time to spread some holiday cheer!

NOTE
If eggnog is out of season, use milk. Vegans and nondairy people: Rejoice, for there are now soy-based nogs on the market.

Right: This pop was frozen in a hemisphere-shaped silicone mold with a playful cocktail stirrer for the stick.

KULFI
(INDIAN FROZEN DAIRY DESSERTS)

Kulfi is served throughout India by street vendors, who take the dessert out of the mold in front of the customer and serve it in a cup. It is then garnished with toppings such as nuts, spices, and rice noodles. Here, I incorporate the toppings into the frozen mixture, add a stick, and freeze it into pop form.

¹/₈ TEASPOON
SAFFRON THREADS

1 TEASPOON CARDAMOM
SEEDS, GROUND

1 (14-OUNCE) CAN
EVAPORATED MILK

1 (14-OUNCE) CAN
SWEETENED
CONDENSED MILK

1 CUP HEAVY CREAM

¹/₂ CUP UNSALTED
PISTACHIOS, CHOPPED

¹/₂ CUP UNSALTED
CASHEWS, CHOPPED

¹/₄ CUP GOLDEN RAISINS

2 TABLESPOONS HONEY

*Makes six 8-ounce pops
or eight 6-ounce pops*

1. In a microwave oven, heat 2 tablespoons water in a small bowl for 30 seconds. Stir in the saffron threads. Add the cardamom. Set aside.
2. In a pitcher, combine the evaporated milk, sweetened condensed milk, and cream. Add the saffron mixture and stir to combine.
3. Pour the mixture into pop molds until one third full. Add some of the nuts and raisins until the molds are two thirds full. Insert the sticks and freeze for 2 hours.
4. Remove from the freezer and add the remaining milk mixture and raisins. Set aside some of the remaining nuts for garnish, and add the rest to the molds. Freeze for at least 6 hours.
5. Remove from the freezer; let stand at room temperature for 5 minutes before removing the pops from the molds.
6. Dip the rim and tip of each pop into honey and press the reserved nuts onto the honey. Surprise your friends with this international treat.

BASMATI RICE PUDDING POPS

3 CUPS MILK

1 CUP HEAVY CREAM

5 BAY LEAVES

5 TABLESPOONS BASMATI RICE

1/3 CUP SUGAR

3 TABLESPOONS GOLDEN RAISINS

2 TEASPOONS PURE VANILLA EXTRACT

2 TEASPOONS GRATED ORANGE ZEST

1/4 CUP PINE NUTS

Makes six 8-ounce pops or eight 6-ounce pops

In Thailand and Malaysia rice pudding is made with black rice, in the Middle East saffron and rosewater are added, and in India rice pudding is studded with nuts. In Latin America rice pudding made with coconut milk is even frozen into pops. Try unusual rices, spices, and sweeteners to give your own pops a unique cultural flair. This recipe and its variations highlight my favorite aspects of many different rice puddings.

1. In a saucepan, combine the milk, cream, and bay leaves and bring to a boil over medium heat. Reduce the heat to maintain a simmer and sprinkle in the rice. Cook, stirring occasionally, for about 40 minutes, until the mixture thickens.
2. Add the sugar and raisins. Cook, stirring, for 5 minutes, or until the sugar is dissolved and the raisins are plump. Remove from the heat and discard the bay leaves.
3. Stir in the vanilla extract, orange zest, and pine nuts. Refrigerate for 10 minutes.
4. Pour into the pop molds. Insert the sticks. Freeze for at least 8 hours.
5. Remove from the freezer; let stand at room temperature for 5 minutes before removing the pops from the molds. Turn on some multiculti pop music and serve.

ALT POPS!
Apple Rice Pudding Pops: Replace the pine nuts with 1/2 cup diced apple. Omit the orange zest. Add 1/2 teaspoon cinnamon.
Orange & Ginger Rice Pudding Pops: Soak the raisins in 1/4 cup fresh orange juice for 1 hour. Drain and add the raisins in step 2. Add 1/2 teaspoon ground ginger.

Opposite: These pops were formed in trapezoid-shaped silicone molds. The grains of rice, raisins, and pine nuts add texture.

FLAN (CRÈME CARAMEL) POPS

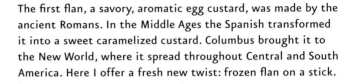

**CARAMEL TOPPING
(INCLUDED IN FLAN
MIX BOX)**

**1 (12-OUNCE) BOX
FLAN MIX**

MILK (SEE NOTE)

3 TABLESPOONS HONEY

*Makes six 8-ounce pops
or eight 6-ounce pops*

The first flan, a savory, aromatic egg custard, was made by the ancient Romans. In the Middle Ages the Spanish transformed it into a sweet caramelized custard. Columbus brought it to the New World, where it spread throughout Central and South America. Here I offer a fresh new twist: frozen flan on a stick.

1. Pour half of the caramel topping into the pop molds. Reserve the rest.
2. In a saucepan, bring the flan mix, milk, and honey to a boil over medium heat. Remove from the heat. Let cool and thicken for a few minutes, then pour into the molds before the mixture turns to pudding. Insert the sticks. Put in the refrigerator for 1 hour, then freeze for at least 8 hours.
3. Remove from the freezer; let stand at room temperature for 5 minutes before removing the pops from the molds. Remove and pour the remaining caramel on top of the pops. Who knew flan could get any better?

NOTE
Different flan mix brands have different preparation directions. Use the amount of milk recommended on the box.

ALT POPS!
Almond Flan Pops: Add $^1/_2$ cup sliced almonds and 1 teaspoon almond extract to the flan mixture after it is removed from the heat in step 2.
Pear Flan Pops: Add $^1/_2$ cup pear nectar to the molds in step 1 and $^1/_4$ cup pureed pears to the flan mixture after it is removed from the heat in step 2.

**Left: This pop gets its pleated edge from
the silicone cupcake mold it was made in.**

TIRAMISÙ POPS

1 CUP FINE LADYFINGER
COOKIE CRUMBS, PLUS
1 LADYFINGER PER POP

½ CUP BREWED COFFEE

2 CUPS MASCARPONE
CHEESE

2 CUPS HEAVY CREAM

1 CUP CONFECTIONERS'
SUGAR

1 TEASPOON PURE
VANILLA EXTRACT

2 TABLESPOONS DUTCH-
PROCESS COCOA POWDER

*Makes six 8-ounce pops
or eight 6-ounce pops*

Do you have a craving for fancy? In Italian, *tiramisù* means "pick me up" or "make me happy," in tribute to its espresso and chocolate double-threat. The cows that eat a gourmet diet to make mascarpone cheese are pretty happy too. They are typically fed special grasses, herbs, and flowers to make their milk and the resulting cheese more flavorful. If you can find a good local mascarpone, these pops will be even more special.

1. In a bowl, combine the ladyfinger crumbs and coffee and set aside.
2. Stick 1 ladyfinger into the end of each pop stick. Set aside.
3. Put the mascarpone in a food processor or blender and pulse a few times until smooth. Add the cream, confectioners' sugar, and vanilla extract; process until smooth.
4. Pour the mascarpone mixture into each mold until it is one quarter full. Freeze for 1 hour.
5. Remove from the freezer. Divide the ladyfinger-coffee mixture among the molds. Sprinkle with cocoa powder. Fill the molds with the mascarpone mixture. Insert the sticks with the ladyfingers. Sprinkle with more cocoa powder. Freeze for at least 8 hours.
6. Remove from the freezer; let stand at room temperature for 5 minutes before removing the pops from the molds. Serve, and let your guests debate whether it's the chocolate, the espresso, or the mascarpone that's making them so giddy.

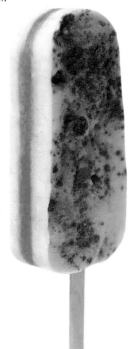

COCONUT CREAM YOGURT POPS

1 1/2 CUPS SWEETENED
SHREDDED COCONUT

3 CUPS VANILLA YOGURT

1/2 CUP MILK

1/3 CUP PLUS ABOUT
2 TABLESPOONS HONEY

*Makes six 8-ounce pops
or eight 6-ounce pops*

It's fun to take healthy yogurt and transform it as it chills into a seemingly decadent dessert. These yogurt pops are inspired by coconut cream and banana cream pie. Vary the flavors with unusual honeys such as sage, orange blossom, or blackberry.

1. Preheat the oven to 350 degrees F. Spread the coconut on a baking sheet and toast it for 7 minutes.

2. In a blender, process the yogurt, milk, and the 1/3 cup honey until smooth. Stir in 1 cup of the toasted coconut.

3. Pour the yogurt mixture into the pop molds. Insert the sticks. Freeze for at least 8 hours.

4. Dab some of the remaining honey onto the pops. Pat the remaining toasted coconut onto the pops. Serve, and don't forget it's yogurt— you and your guests should feel free to have two apiece.

ALT POPS!
Banana & Nut Yogurt Pops: Replace the coconut with 1 cup mashed bananas. Finely chop 1/4 cup walnuts and pat them onto the pops in step 4.
Chocolate & Banana Yogurt Pops: Replace the coconut with 1 cup mashed bananas. Stir in 1/2 cup chocolate chips after blending the yogurt mixture. Pat finely chopped chocolate chips onto the pops in step 4.

**Opposite: This fancy-looking pop was made in a modest paper cup.
A cocktail pick stick and shredded coconut topping dress it up.**

ROCKY ROAD PUDDING POPS

1 CUP SUGAR

1/4 CUP DUTCH-PROCESS COCOA POWDER

3/4 CUP CORNSTARCH

1/4 TEASPOON SALT

4 CUPS MILK

4 TABLESPOONS UNSALTED BUTTER

2 TEASPOONS PURE VANILLA EXTRACT

3/4 CUP MINI MARSHMALLOWS

3/4 CUP CHOPPED WALNUTS

Makes six 8-ounce pops or eight 6-ounce pops

This chocolate, marshmallow, and walnut combination has always been one of my favorites. Sink your teeth into the *Rocky Road Pudding Pop* (front and center in photo) or try the *Pistachio Pudding Pop, Butterscotch Pudding Pop,* or *White Chocolate Macadamia Nut Pudding Pop* (back row, from left to right).

1. In a saucepan, combine the sugar, cocoa powder, cornstarch, and salt.
2. Add the milk and bring to a boil over medium heat, stirring constantly, for 5 to 7 minutes. Remove from the heat as soon as the mixture thickens.
3. Stir in the butter until melted. Add the vanilla extract. Refrigerate for 10 minutes, until cool but not thickened.
4. Stir in the marshmallows and walnuts.
5. Pour into pop molds. Insert the sticks. Freeze for at least 8 hours.
6. Remove from the freezer; let stand at room temperature for 5 minutes before removing the pops from the molds. Serve, and see if your road doesn't become smoother by the minute!

ALT POPS!

Pistachio Pudding Pops: Omit the cocoa powder and marshmallows. Replace the walnuts with 1 1/2 cups shelled pistachios. In a food processor or blender, grind 3/4 cup of the pistachios to a paste. Stir the pistachio paste and pistachios into the pudding in step 2. Add 3 drops green food coloring in step 4.

Butterscotch Pudding Pops: Omit the cocoa powder, marshmallows, and walnuts. Use brown sugar instead of granulated sugar. Stir 1 cup butterscotch chips into the mixture in step 4.

Chocolate Pudding Pops: Replace the marshmallows and walnuts with 3/4 cup chocolate chips.

White Chocolate & Macadamia Nut Pudding Pops: Omit the cocoa powder. Replace the walnuts with macadamia nuts. Add 3/4 cup white chocolate chips in step 4.

Chapter 5

COFFEE & TEA POPS

If you're like me, when the mood for coffee or tea strikes, the craving must be satisfied—immediately. It probably comes as no surprise that for much of its history coffee was considered a spiritual drink used in religious ceremonies and that, due to its medicinal properties, tea is known in many cultures as "the elixir of life." You've likely developed strong preferences about how your coffee and tea drinks are served—straight black or gussied up with syrups and creams or lemon and mint, hot out of the pot or poured over ice. These *Coffee & Tea Pops* offer new ways to enjoy all the flavors that can be derived from the coffee bean and tea leaf. Best of all, while a hot cup of coffee or tea is at its peak for only a few minutes, *Coffee & Tea Pops* maintain their rich flavor through your very last lick.

Opposite: *Thai Iced Coffee* and *Thai Iced Tea Pops* (see page 89 for the recipes).

MOCHA POPS

3 CUPS MILK

1 CUP GOOD-QUALITY
CHOCOLATE SYRUP

1/4 CUP SUGAR

1/4 TEASPOON CINNAMON

1/2 CUP HEAVY CREAM

1 TEASPOON PURE
VANILLA EXTRACT

8 SHOTS HOT FRESHLY
BREWED ESPRESSO
(OR 3 CUPS DOUBLE-
STRENGTH BREWED
COFFEE)

1/2 CUP GRATED SEMISWEET
CHOCOLATE AND/OR
CHOCOLATE-COVERED
ESPRESSO BEANS

*Makes six 8-ounce pops
or eight 6-ounce pops*

Even after I discovered the joy of unadulterated espresso, chocolate and coffee was still one of my favorite combinations, and it works especially well in these *Mocha Pops*. The caffeine in the chocolate and the espresso provides a double jolt. Try adding chocolate chips or almonds for even more flavor.

1. In a saucepan, combine the milk, chocolate syrup, sugar, and 1/8 teaspoon of the cinnamon and cook, stirring constantly, over low heat for 5 minutes. Remove from the heat and stir in the cream and vanilla extract. Let cool.
2. Add the espresso. Let cool.
3. Stir in the chocolate and/or the chocolate-covered espresso beans.
4. Pour the mixture into the pop molds. Insert the sticks. Freeze for at least 6 hours.
5. Remove from the freezer; let stand at room temperature for 5 minutes before removing the pops from the molds. Serve to your chocolate- and coffee-addicted friends.

ALT POPS!
Peppermint Mocha Pop: In step 3, add 1/4 cup crushed peppermint candies.
Mexican Mocha Pops: In step 1, add 1/8 teaspoon freshly grated nutmeg and replace the vanilla extract with almond extract. In step 3, add 1/4 cup ground almonds.

Left: This fun pop was made by alternating mocha ice cubes with sweetened cream ice cubes on a coffee stirrer.

THAI ICED COFFEE POPS

½ CUP SWEETENED
CONDENSED MILK,
OR TO TASTE

½ CUP EVAPORATED
MILK

½ CUP MILK

2 CUPS THAI COFFEE
POWDER (SEE NOTE)

½ TEASPOON
CARDAMOM SEEDS

CRUSHED ICE

*Makes six 8-ounce pops
or eight 6-ounce pops*

Thai iced coffee is a very sweet, creamy refreshment brewed by street vendors in a cloth bag and served in a plastic bag with plenty of crushed ice and a straw. These *Thai Iced Coffee Pops*, pictured on page 86, are based on traditional recipes and serving methods. The Thai coffee powder (*oliang*) and the milk are poured over crushed ice and not mixed, creating one tasty layer on top of another.

1. In a small bowl, combine 6 tablespoons of the sweetened condensed milk with the evaporated milk and regular milk. Stir well and set aside.
2. Bring 4½ cups water to a boil in a saucepan. Spoon the coffee powder and cardamom into a cheesecloth bag or coffee filter. Close securely with kitchen string and place the bag in a heat-resistant pitcher. Pour the boiling water over the bag, then sweeten to taste with the remaining sweetened condensed milk. Stir well. Let sit for 10 minutes, until dark brown, then discard the bag.
3. Fill each mold halfway with crushed ice. Pour in the milk mixture until one third full. Freeze for at least 20 minutes.
4. Remove from the freezer. Fill the molds with the Thai coffee mixture. Freeze for at least 6 hours.
5. Remove from the freezer; let stand at room temperature for 5 minutes before removing the pops from the molds. Enjoy as an afternoon pick-me-up.

NOTE
Each brand of Thai coffee or iced tea powder calls for a different powder-to-water ratio. Read the directions on the package to adjust this recipe as needed. If the directions are written in Thai, try the ratios here, then adjust the amounts the next time if necessary.

ALT POPS!
Thai Iced Tea Pops: Replace the coffee powder with ¾ cup Thai iced tea powder. Stir until the mixture is orangish brown. Proceed with the *Thai Iced Coffee Pops* method.

CARAMEL LATTE POPS

**6 OR 8 SHOTS FRESHLY
BREWED ESPRESSO, OR
MORE IF DESIRED**

4 1/2 CUPS MILK

1/4 CUP CARAMEL SAUCE

**1/4 CUP FINELY DICED
SOFT CARAMEL CANDIES**

*Makes six 8-ounce pops
or eight 6-ounce pops*

I lived in Seattle in the early nineties when some of the major coffee brands were exploding. I diligently mapped out my commute so I could enjoy lattes from each place. This effort paid off when I was hired to design a chain of coffee shops—and unique latte drinks—in Alaska. These *Caramel Latte Pops* are based on those recipes. Remember to be generous with the shots. BuzzBuzzBuzz.

1. Put the espresso in a bowl.
2. Stir in the milk, caramel sauce, and caramel candies.
3. Pour the mixture into the pop molds. Insert the sticks. Freeze for at least 6 hours.
4. Remove from the freezer; let stand at room temperature for 5 minutes before removing the pops from the molds. Serve—but be sure you always have some of these in the freezer for latte emergencies.

ALT POPS!
Classic Latte Pops: Omit the caramel sauce and candies.
Eggnog Latte Pops: Replace the milk with eggnog and 1 teaspoon cinnamon. Omit the caramel sauce and candies.
Espresso Pops: Use 4 shots of espresso per pop and omit all other ingredients.
Kahlúa Coffee & Cream Pops: Replace the caramel sauce with Kahlúa and half of the milk with cream. Replace the caramel candies with brown sugar.
Irish Cream Coffee Pops: Use 5 cups freshly brewed double-strength coffee. Use 1 1/2 cups milk and replace the caramel sauce and candies with 2 tablespoons Irish cream Italian syrup.
Hazelnut Coffee Pops: Use the *Irish Cream Coffee Pops* variation, replacing the Irish cream syrup with hazelnut syrup. Add 1/3 cup chopped hazelnuts in step 3.

Opposite: Make these pops in espresso cups for authentic café flair. Here is an assortment to suit different tastes (clockwise from front): *Espresso Pop, Caramel Latte Pop,* and *Classic Latte Pop.*

SPICED ORANGE COFFEE POPS

1 CUP GROUND COFFEE

ZEST OF 1 ORANGE,
CUT OFF IN A LONG,
CONTINUOUS SPIRAL

2 TEASPOONS CINNAMON

1 CUP FRESH ORANGE
JUICE

1/2 CUP PACKED BROWN
SUGAR

3/4 CUP MILK

3/4 CUP DRAINED CANNED
MANDARIN ORANGES

1 1/2 CUPS WHIPPED
CREAM

*Makes six 8-ounce pops
or eight 6-ounce pops*

I love the refreshing flavors of fruits mixed with the strong, rich flavor of coffee. Store-bought flavored coffees are made with extracts that are infused in the beans while they are roasted. That is all well and good, but extracts tend to taste more like candy flavorings than actual fruit. These pops are made with unflavored beans combined with real fruit, juices, and spices. The whipped cream transforms them into an indulgent dessert.

1. Put the coffee, orange zest, and 1 1/2 teaspoons of the cinnamon in a coffee filter. Put the orange juice in the empty pot of the coffee maker. Brew coffee, using 3 1/2 cups water.
2. Stir the brown sugar into the coffee and orange juice mixture until dissolved. Stir in the milk.
3. Divide the mandarin orange segments among the pop molds. Pour the coffee mixture into the molds. Insert the sticks. Freeze for at least 6 hours.
4. Remove from the freezer; let stand at room temperature for 5 minutes before removing the pops from the molds. Top with whipped cream. Sprinkle with the remaining 1/2 teaspoon cinnamon. Prepare to be wowed.

ALT POPS!
Raspberry Coffee Pops: Replace the orange juice with raspberry juice. Replace the mandarin orange segments with raspberries. The orange zest is optional. Omit the cinnamon.
Cherry Coffee Pops: Replace the orange juice with cherry juice, and the oranges with cherries. Omit the orange zest and cinnamon.

COFFEE GRANITAS
(ITALIAN FLAVORED FROZEN ICES)

4 1/2 CUPS FRESHLY
BREWED ESPRESSO OR
DOUBLE-STRENGTH
COFFEE

1 CUP SUGAR

2 CUPS WHIPPED CREAM
(OPTIONAL)

5 TABLESPOONS SHAVED
CHOCOLATE (OPTIONAL)

Serves 4

Although traditionally coffee flavored and eaten for breakfast with a brioche, granitas are now made in many fruit flavors and served as dessert. Most granitas are mixed with a whisk as they freeze so that the mixture forms larger individual ice crystals. In some regions of Italy, the flavoring syrup is drizzled over a block of plain ice and the flavor is mixed in as the ice is shaved. Coffee granitas are served in a tall glass and topped with whipped cream.

1. In a bowl, combine the hot espresso and the sugar and stir until dissolved. Pour into a 9-by-13-inch baking dish and cover with plastic wrap. Freeze for 45 minutes.
2. With a whisk, distribute the frozen crystals. Cover and freeze again for 45 minutes.
3. Whisk again. Freeze for 3 hours, until frozen.
4. With an ice scraper or a fork, scrape the ice to break up the crystals. Freeze for 1 hour.
5. Remove from the freezer and scoop the granitas into tall glasses. For breakfast, serve plain; for dessert, top the granitas with the whipped cream and shaved chocolate. Dig in with tall spoons.

OTHER GRANITAS
Tea Granitas: Replace the coffee with your favorite tea. Hibiscus, chai, berry, and green teas all taste good. Whipped cream is optional. Omit the chocolate and top with fresh fruit slices.

MINT TEA POPS

³/₄ CUP SUGAR

¹/₃ CUP CAFFEINE-FREE LOOSE GREEN TEA, OR 5 TEA BAGS

12 SPRIGS FRESH MINT (SEE NOTE)

JUICE OF ¹/₂ LEMON

¹/₂ CUP HONEY, OR TO TASTE

¹/₄ CUP EDIBLE FLOWERS

¹/₄ CUP BLANCHED ALMONDS

Makes six 8-ounce pops or eight 6-ounce pops

I cannot think of a flavor that says cool and refreshing better than mint. Recently I wowed my guests with a *Mint Tea Pops* tasting party where I served an array of pops, from spearmint to chocolate mint, all made from herbs grown in my garden. All natural and caffeine free, these *Mint Tea Pops* and the herb tea variations are also transparent, making them fantastic for showcasing frozen and suspended leaves, flowers, and fruit.

1. Bring 4¹/₂ cups water to a boil in a saucepan. Pour into a heat-resistant pitcher with the sugar and stir to dissolve.
2. Add the tea, 10 of the mint sprigs, and the lemon juice. Cover and let steep for 1 hour.
3. Pour through a fine-mesh sieve into a bowl and stir in honey to taste.
4. Add a few fresh mint leaves, flowers, and almonds to each pop mold. Pour in the tea and insert the sticks. Freeze for at least 6 hours.
5. Remove from the freezer; let stand at room temperature for 5 minutes before removing the pops from the molds. Cool off with this minty pop.

NOTE
If you don't have fresh mint, ¹/₃ cup loose mint tea or 5 mint tea bags can be substituted for the mint and green tea.

ALT POPS!
Chamomile Tea Pops: Replace the mint sprigs with 8 fresh chamomile sprigs. If the chamomile has flowers, reserve the flowers to add to the molds in step 4. Add ¹/₄ cup sliced almonds after the honey in step 3.
Lavender Tea Pops: Replace the mint sprigs with 4 fresh lavender sprigs. Add ¹/₄ cup sliced almonds after the honey in step 3.
Sage Tea Pops: Replace the mint sprigs with 6 fresh sage sprigs. Replace the lemon juice with the juice of 1 orange. Add ¹/₄ cup dried currants after the honey in step 3.

SOUTHERN SWEET TEA POPS

1 3/4 CUPS SUGAR

6 PEACHES, CUT INTO
WEDGES, SKIN ON

2 LIMES, PEELED AND
CUT INTO ROUNDS

1 SPRIG OF FRESH MINT

3 "FAMILY-SIZE" OR
8 REGULAR-SIZED
BAGS ORANGE PEKOE
BLACK TEA

*Makes six 8-ounce pops
or eight 6-ounce pops*

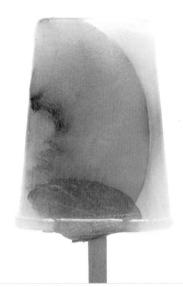

I created these pops as a reminder of all things Southern: hiking beneath moss-covered oak trees, crossing paths with alligators, and eating at simple home-style restaurants that serve bottomless glasses of Southern sweet tea. The sweetener is added to the tea before it is chilled, either during or after brewing. Southerners add peaches and other local fruits to further flavor the tea. Some insist that the best sweet tea is brewed from the heat of the sun. That's how I prepare these *Southern Sweet Tea Pops*.

1. In a saucepan over low heat, bring 2 cups water to a simmer and stir in the sugar until the sugar is dissolved. Remove from the heat and add 2 cups cold water. Let cool for 10 minutes.
2. Pour the sugar water into a clear glass container. Add the peaches, limes, and mint and stir. Add the tea bags. Cover and put the container outside in the sun for 3 to 5 hours, or until the tea reaches your desired strength.
3. Remove the tea bags and stir the tea. Scoop out the peaches, limes, and mint, and divide them evenly among the pop molds. Pour in the tea. Insert the sticks. Freeze for at least 6 hours.
4. Remove from the freezer; let stand at room temperature for 5 minutes before removing the pops from the molds. Serve graciously.

ALT POPS!
Southern Sweet Plum Tea Pops: Replace the peaches with plums and the limes with 1 lemon.
Southern Sweet Fig Tea Pops: Replace the peaches with stemmed fresh figs.

SWEDISH BERRY TEA POPS

3 CUPS HOT BREWED
LINGONBERRY TEA
(MADE WITH 3 TEA BAGS)

1 1/2 CUPS HOT
BREWED HIBISCUS TEA
(MADE WITH 1 TEA BAG)

3/4 CUP SUGAR

1/4 CUP RAISINS

1/3 CUP BLUEBERRIES

1/3 CUP RASPBERRIES

1/3 CUP FRESH
LINGONBERRIES
(OPTIONAL)

*Makes six 8-ounce pops
or eight 6-ounce pops*

Lingonberries are wild berries found in northern Europe. They are similar to cranberries but sweeter and not as tart. They are rarely cultivated but harvested from forests in the Swedish high country. Lingonberry tea pairs beautifully with the hibiscus tea in this recipe; substitute other berries for the fresh blueberries and raspberries if you like. Serve these pops alongside Swedish pancakes and meatballs.

1. Pour the hot teas and the sugar into a heatproof pitcher. Stir to dissolve the sugar.
2. Gently stir in the raisins, blueberries, raspberries, and ligonberries, if using.
3. Pour into pop molds. Insert the sticks. Freeze for at least 8 hours.
4. Remove from the freezer; let stand at room temperature for 5 minutes before removing the pops from the molds. Throw a tea party with a twist.

ALT POPS!
Hibiscus Tea Pops: Replace the lingonberry tea with 4 cups hibiscus tea (made with 4 tea bags). Replace the berries with 2 sliced limes. Add 1/4 cup lime juice and, if you like, 1/8 cup dried hibiscus flowers.
Swedish Berry Herb Pops: Replace the hibiscus tea with mint tea. Replace the raisins with dried currants. Add 1 tablespoon chopped fresh mint and 1 tablespoon chopped rosemary.

LYCHEE BUBBLE "BOBA" TEA POPS

½ CUP BUBBLE
TAPIOCA PEARLS
(BLACK OR COLORED)

¾ CUP GRANULATED
SUGAR

½ CUP PACKED BROWN
SUGAR

2½ CUPS BREWED TEA
(SUCH AS CHINA BLACK,
JASMINE, LYCHEE, OR
GREEN), COOLED TO
ROOM TEMPERATURE

½ CUP UNSWEETENED
COCONUT MILK

1 CUP LYCHEE JUICE

¼ CUP DICED LYCHEE

¼ CUP COCONUT JELLY,
CUT INTO PIECES
(AVAILABLE AT ASIAN
GROCERIES)

*Makes six 8-ounce pops
or eight 6-ounce pops*

Recently, bubble teas—sweet, refreshing flavored drinks, often with large tapioca pearls at the bottom of the cup—have become all the rage (though they had been popular among Asian schoolchildren since the eighties). They make great pops: As each pearl is revealed, you experience a fun chewy sensation. There are hundreds of bubble tea flavors that would make great pops: shown opposite, from left to right, are *Almond, Taro,* and *Lychee Bubble Tea Pops.*

1. In a saucepan, bring 5 cups water to a boil. Add the tapioca pearls. Boil for 30 minutes, covered (or according to the directions on the package). Turn off the heat and let sit for 30 minutes, or until soft. Rinse and drain. Set aside.
2. In a separate saucepan, combine the granulated sugar, brown sugar, and 2 cups water. Cook over medium heat, stirring, until the sugar is dissolved.
3. In a bowl, combine the tea, sugar water, coconut milk, and lychee juice.
4. Divide the diced lychee, coconut jelly, and tapioca pearls among the pop molds. Pour the tea mixture into the molds. Insert the sticks. Freeze for at least 6 hours.
5. Remove from the freezer; let stand at room temperature for 5 minutes before removing the pops from the molds. Delight your friends with this surprising pop.

ALT POPS!
Fruit Bubble Tea Pops: Replace the lychee juice and fruit with your favorite juice and fruit.
Taro Bubble Tea Pops: Omit the coconut milk and jelly, lychee juice, and lychee. Add ¼ cup taro powder and 2 additional cups tea.
Almond Bubble Tea Pops: Omit the coconut milk and jelly, lychee juice, and lychee. Stir in 1½ cups milk, ¼ cup almond powder, and ¼ cup chopped almonds in step 4.

GREEN TEA POPS

3 TABLESPOONS MATCHA (GREEN TEA POWDER; SEE NOTE)

1 CUP SUGAR

2 CUPS MILK

2 CUPS HEAVY CREAM

2 TEASPOONS PURE VANILLA EXTRACT

Makes six 8-ounce pops or eight 6-ounce pops

Matcha is the green tea powder used in Japanese tea ceremonies. It takes a lifetime to learn the proper methods of preparing and drinking the ceremonial tea, but these light, sweet pops—a playful interpretation of the traditional flavors—can be enjoyed by novices any time.

1. In a saucepan, bring $1/2$ cup water to a boil. In a small bowl, combine the boiling water, green tea powder, and $3/4$ cup of the sugar, stirring to dissolve the sugar. Stir in the milk.
2. In a large bowl, whip the cream, vanilla extract, and remaining $1/4$ cup sugar until the cream just starts to thicken, 1 to 2 minutes.
3. Gently fold the milk mixture into the whipped cream.
4. Pour the mixture into the pop molds. Insert the sticks. Freeze for at least 10 hours.
5. Remove from the freezer; let stand at room temperature for 5 minutes before removing the pops from the molds. Create your own tea pop ceremony.

NOTE
Matcha can be found in most Asian grocery stores.

ALT POPS!
Green Tea & Red Bean Pops: Red bean paste can be purchased prepackaged. Add the tea mixture to the molds until two thirds full, then freeze until firm. Add the bean paste, top them off with more tea mixture, and freeze until firm.

Left: These dainty green tea pops were formed in flower-shaped ice cube trays. Bamboo sticks are the perfect finishing touch.

MASALA CHAI TEA POPS

8 WHITE OR GREEN CARDAMOM PODS, CRUSHED

4 WHOLE CLOVES

1 CINNAMON STICK, CRUSHED

1/4 TEASPOON FRESHLY GROUND BLACK PEPPER

1 TEASPOON PEELED AND CHOPPED FRESH GINGER

2 CUPS MILK

4 TABLESPOONS SUGAR

4 TEASPOONS LOOSE ASSAM BLACK TEA OR ENGLISH BREAKFAST TEA

Makes six 8-ounce pops or eight 6-ounce pops

Chai is made by steeping loose-leaf black leaf tea in a pot with water, milk, sweetener, and ground masala—a blend of spices that usually contains cardamom. In India, *chaiwallahs* (chai street vendors) carry pots of chai and serve it in freshly fired earthen cups, pouring it from a great height to aerate the chai. Here the warm, spicy flavors of masala chai are transformed into frozen pops.

1. In a saucepan, combine 4 cups water, the cardamom, cloves, cinnamon, pepper, and ginger. Bring to a boil over high heat, then lower the heat, cover, and simmer for 7 minutes.
2. Add the milk and sugar, then simmer for 3 minutes. Remove from the heat.
3. Add the tea leaves. Cover and let steep for 3 to 4 minutes. Pour through a fine-mesh sieve into a bowl and let the chai mixture cool to room temperature.
4. Fill the pop molds with the mixture. Insert the sticks. Freeze for at least 6 hours.
5. Remove from the freezer; let stand at room temperature for 5 minutes before removing the pops from the molds. Enjoy this spicy-delicious pop.

CUSTOMIZE YOUR CHAI
Indian families often develop their own traditional family recipes for chai. Following is a list of spices and sweeteners commonly used. Experiment to create your own Chai Ice Pops recipe.

Common Chai Tea Spices: cardamom, ginger, black pepper, cinnamon, star anise, cloves, nutmeg, coriander, allspice, chocolate, cocoa powder, vanilla, licorice, fennel, saffron.
Common Chai Sweeteners: granulated sugar, molasses, honey, jaggery.

Left: This *Masala Chai Tea Pop* **was made from a folded waxed paper mold. The stick is a bamboo cocktail pick.**

Chapter 6

COCKTAIL
POPS

Even with competition from seasonal diversions like fireworks, swimming pools, county fairs, block parties, and barbecues, these *Cocktail Pops* could be voted summer's favorite pastime. Inspired by traditional mixed drinks, they are sweet and cool, and a wonderful way to break the ice at a warm-weather shindig. Whip up and freeze a few batches of *Cocktail Pops* ahead of time so you can engage in witty conversation with your guests all evening and not concern yourself with such drink-making details as shakers and strainers and swizzle sticks. These striking pops—bright *Blue Lagoon Pops*, chic *Sweet Martini Pops* (complete with olives), and kitchy *Mai Tai Pops*—can be served on platters alongside traditional party hors d'oeuvres or presented solo, in buckets or tubs of ice.

Opposite: These *Tequila Sunrise* and *Sunset Pops* were made in tall shot glasses. Cocktail stirrers serve as the sticks. (See page 104 for recipes.)

TEQUILA SUNRISE POPS

1 ORANGE, PEELED AND CUT INTO THIN SLICES

1/4 CUP TEQUILA

3 CUPS FRESH ORANGE JUICE

STEMMED MARASCHINO CHERRIES (1 PER POP)

1/4 CUP GRENADINE

Makes 24 two-ounce ice cube–tray pops, six 8-ounce pops, or eight 6-ounce pops

No matter the time of day, it's happy hour when you serve these scrumptious *Tequila Sunrise Pops*. The grenadine and orange juice combine to create beautiful, icy color gradations that mimic a sunrise. Pair with the *Tequila Sunset* variation if you want to really impress your guests.

1. In a small bowl, combine the orange slices and tequila. Let sit for 10 minutes.
2. In a pitcher, combine the orange slices and the orange juice.
3. Put a cherry in each pop mold. Fill the molds three quarters full with the orange juice mixture. Put in the freezer for 20 minutes, until slushy.
4. Remove from the freezer. Divide the grenadine among the molds. Insert the sticks. Freeze for at least 12 hours.
5. Remove from the freezer; let stand at room temperature for 5 minutes before removing the pops from the molds. Serve these pops whenever you choose.

ALT POPS!
Tequila Sunset Pops: Replace the grenadine with 1/4 cup blackberry juice and 5 tablespoons blackberry brandy. Replace the cherries with fresh blackberries.

Opposite: These pops were made in gem-shaped silicone molds with cocktail stirrers for sticks.

MARGARITA POPS

1 LIME, PEELED AND CUT INTO THIN SLICES

1/2 LEMON, PEELED, SEEDED, AND CUT INTO THIN SLICES

1 1/2 CUPS FRESH LIME JUICE

1 1/2 CUPS FRESH LEMON JUICE

5 TABLESPOONS TRIPLE SEC

2 TABLESPOONS TEQUILA

1 1/2 CUPS ICE CUBES

1/4 CUP LIGHT CORN SYRUP

SALT FOR THE POP RIMS (OPTIONAL)

Makes 24 two-ounce ice cube–tray pops, six 8-ounce pops, or eight 6-ounce pops

Margarita Pops don't need to be reserved for invited guests. These are a staple at our house, always waiting for us to enjoy out on the patio after a long day. I prefer mine dipped in salt, as described in the recipe below; my husband enjoys his on the rocks, without. We pair them with our favorite Mexican dishes: tacos, carnitas, enchiladas, and carne asada.

1. In a food processor or blender, combine the lime and lemon slices and juices, triple sec, tequila, and ice cubes. Process until smooth.
2. Fill the pop molds with the mixture. Insert the sticks. Freeze for at least 12 hours.
3. Remove from the freezer; let stand at room temperature for 5 minutes before removing the pops from the molds.
4. Brush corn syrup on the rim of each pop. Dip the rim into salt (to taste). Serve these pops on a plate of rock salt.

MIMOSA POPS

**3 CUPS FRESH
ORANGE JUICE,
BLOOD ORANGE JUICE,
OR TANGERINE JUICE**

**4 TABLESPOONS
GRENADINE**

JUICE OF 1 LEMON

1 CUP CHAMPAGNE

**STEMMED MARASCHINO
CHERRIES (1 PER POP)**

**1 ORANGE, PEELED AND
CUT INTO THIN ROUNDS**

*Makes 24 two-ounce
ice cube–tray pops,
six 8-ounce pops,
or eight 6-ounce pops*

Lounging with friends and savoring *Mimosa Pops* sums up everything I love about hosting a weekend brunch. As guests arrive, I offer this little touch of decadence to start the party with a smile. Try using blood orange juice or tangerine juice for an exotic, tangy twist.

1. Pour the orange juice, grenadine, lemon juice, and Champagne into a pitcher. Stir, then let sit for 5 minutes.
2. Put a cherry and an orange round into each mold. Pour the orange juice mixture into the molds. Insert the sticks.
3. Freeze for at least 12 hours.
4. Remove from the freezer; let stand at room temperature for 5 minutes before removing the pops from the molds. Time to charm your brunch guests!

ALT POPS!
Pineapple & Orange Mimosa Pops: Use 1¹/₂ cups orange juice and 1¹/₂ cups pineapple juice.
Orange & Peach Mimosa Pops: Use 1¹/₂ cups orange juice and 1¹/₂ cups peach nectar.
Screwdriver Pops: Substitute 5 tablespoons vodka for the Champagne.
Amaretto & Orange Pops: Substitute 6 tablespoons amaretto for the Champagne. Add 2 tablespoons sliced almonds.

Opposite: This little *Sangria Pop* (bottom) and *Mimosa Pop* (top) were created in ice cube trays converted to pop molds. To learn how, see **Mini Ice Pop Mold, page 120.**

SANGRIA POPS

1 GRANNY SMITH APPLE, DICED

1 PEAR, DICED

1 PEACH, DICED

¼ CUP BRANDY

¼ CUP RUM

2½ CUPS DRY RED WINE

½ CUP SUPERFINE SUGAR

JUICE OF 1 LEMON

JUICE OF 2 LIMES

1 CUP FRESH ORANGE JUICE

1 CUP SELTZER

½ TEASPOON CINNAMON

Makes 24 two-ounce ice cube–tray pops, six 8-ounce pops, or eight 6-ounce pops

Friends flip over these *Sangria Pops*, inspired by the classic Spanish fiesta drink. Sangria is easy to freeze because the fruit absorbs most of the alcohol and the liquids surrounding the fruit freeze well. Feel free to use different types of wines and fruits to create your own variations.

1. Put the apple, pear, and peach in a pitcher. Pour the brandy and rum over the fruit. Let sit for 15 minutes. Add the wine and put in the refrigerator for 2 hours.
2. Stir in the superfine sugar, lemon juice, lime juice, orange juice, seltzer, and cinnamon.
3. Fill the pop molds with the mixture. Insert the sticks. Freeze for at least 12 hours.
4. Remove from the freezer; let stand at room temperature for 5 minutes before removing the pops from the molds. Cheers!

ALT POPS!
Sangria Blanca Pops: Replace the red wine with dry white wine. Replace the orange juice with white grape juice. Add ³/₄ cup white grapes.

COSMOPOLITAN POPS

6 OR 8 SLICES PEELED LIME

2 1/2 CUPS CRANBERRY JUICE

5 TABLESPOONS TRIPLE SEC

1 CUP FRESH LIME JUICE

5 TABLESPOONS COINTREAU

1/4 CUP VODKA

1 1/2 CUPS CRUSHED ICE

LIME SLICES FOR GARNISH

Makes 24 two-ounce ice cube–tray pops, six 8-ounce pops, or eight 6-ounce pops

Cosmopolitan Pops are a tasty twist on the glamorous drink. Created recently in bartending history, the Cosmo grew quickly in popularity in the late eighties and nineties. Bartenders claim that women order them not because they like the sweet-tart taste but because they like how they look holding a cocktail glass in their hand. I think we look just as good holding these pops.

1. Put a lime slice in each pop mold. (Omit if you are making ice cube–tray pops.)
2. Combine all of the ingredients except the lime garnish in a pitcher.
3. Pour into the pop molds. Insert the sticks. Freeze for at least 12 hours.
4. Remove from the freezer. Place a lime slice on each stick. Let stand at room temperature for 5 minutes before removing the pops from the molds. Enjoy at cocktail hour or while lounging by the pool.

ALT POPS!
Champagne Cosmopolitan Pops: Reduce the cranberry juice to 1 1/4 cups, use 1/2 lemon slice in each pop, and omit the vodka. Add 1 1/2 cups Champagne and 1/4 cup fresh cranberries in step 2.
Anisette Cosmopolitan Pop: Omit the Cointreau. Soak 1/4 cup fresh cranberries in 5 tablespoons anisette and add them in step 2. Dip the pops in anisette right before serving.

Opposite: To achieve this whimsical martini glass shape, these pops were made in a funnel with a cocktail stirrer for a stick.

MOJITO POPS

1 1/2 CUPS FRESH LIME JUICE

2 1/2 CUPS CLUB SODA

1/3 CUP FRESH MINT LEAVES

1 LEMON, PEELED AND CUT INTO WEDGES

3 LIMES, PEELED AND CUT INTO WEDGES

1 1/2 CUPS SUGAR

4 TABLESPOONS LIGHT RUM

Makes 24 two-ounce ice cube–tray pops, six 8-ounce pops, or eight 6-ounce pops

Mojito Pops are as much fun to make as they are to savor. While preparing these intoxicating Havana Cuban cocktail pops, you get to mash the fruits and herbs with a muddler to release their flavor. These unusual pops are a perfect addition to your next pool party or Caribbean barbecue. They're fantastic with jerk chicken.

1. Pour the lime juice, club soda, and 1 cup water into a pitcher and let sit for 5 minutes.
2. Add the mint, lemon and lime wedges, sugar, and rum to the pitcher. Mash all the ingredients together with a muddler or a wooden spoon.
3. Pour into the pop molds, being sure to distribute the fruits and mint evenly among the molds. Insert the sticks. Freeze for at least 12 hours.
4. Remove from the freezer; let stand at room temperature for 5 minutes before removing the pops from the molds. Kick back and enjoy these lazy-day pops.

ALT POPS!
Mango Mojito Pops: Reduce the club soda to 2 cups. Replace the water with 1 1/2 cups mango nectar. Add 1 peeled sliced mango in step 2.

MAI TAI POPS

2 TABLESPOONS LIGHT RUM

2 TABLESPOONS DARK RUM

3 TABLESPOONS ORANGE CURAÇAO

2½ CUPS FRESH ORANGE JUICE

1¼ CUPS SOUR MIX (LEMON AND LIME JUICES WITH SIMPLE SYRUP)

¼ CUP FRESH LIME JUICE

¼ CUP ORGEAT SYRUP (SEE NOTE) OR ALMOND SYRUP

2 LIMES, UNPEELED, CUT INTO THIN ROUNDS

¼ CUP SLICED ALMONDS

12 FRESH MINT LEAVES

Makes 24 two-ounce ice cube–tray pops, six 8-ounce pops, or eight 6-ounce pops

East meets West in these Polynesian *Mai Tai Pops*. Think hula dancers, orchid leis, flaming torches, and some campy tiki fun. If you are really ambitious and want to create pops you won't find anywhere else, make your own tiki silicone molds (see page 123) to shape these pops. I like to present these pops on a bed of flowers or individually on a small plate next to a single orchid.

1. In a pitcher, combine the rums and curaçao, orange juice, sour mix, lime juice, and orgeat syrup.
2. Reserve 1 lime slice for each pop. Peel the remaining slices. Distribute the almonds, peeled lime slices, and mint leaves evenly among the pop molds.
3. Pour the juice mixture into the molds. Insert the sticks. Freeze for at least 12 hours.
4. Remove from the freezer; let stand at room temperature for 5 minutes before removing the pops from the molds. If you like, stick a reserved lime slice onto each stick for garnish. Let these pops transport you to summer in the South Seas.

NOTE

Orgeat syrup, a classic ingredient in the Mai Tai, is flavored with almonds and rose or orange flower water.

Right: I made the original master pattern for this tiki pop mold from a wax candle, then made deeper carves to give definition to the tiki.

BLUE LAGOON POPS

STEMMED MARASCHINO CHERRIES (1 PER POP)

4 TABLESPOONS VODKA

2 TABLESPOONS BLUE CURAÇAO

¼ CUP LIGHT CORN SYRUP

2½ CUPS LEMONADE

6 DROPS BLUE FOOD COLORING

Makes 24 two-ounce ice cube–tray pops, six 8-ounce pops, or eight 6-ounce pops

These enchanting *Blue Lagoon Pops* will be a standout at any party. Blue curaçao is the elixir responsible for their delightful color, although you can add a little food coloring to play up the blue, if you like. However you achieve it, the cool tone is always a surprise and makes these pops seem especially icy. Consider dropping these little pops in a cocktail for a sweet sensation.

1. In a bowl, combine the cherries and vodka. Let sit for 10 minutes.
2. In a pitcher, combine the curaçao, corn syrup, lemonade, and food coloring.
3. Stick a cherry onto the end of each pop stick or put 1 in each mold. Fill the pop molds with the curaçao mixture. Insert the sticks. Freeze for at least 12 hours.
4. Remove from the freezer; let stand at room temperature for 5 minutes before removing the pops from the molds. Enjoy playing bartender when you serve these truly stunning pops.

Above: These pops were made in Mini Ice Pop Molds that I made from ice cube trays. (See page 120 for instructions.)

BLUE HAWAIIAN SNOW CONES

1/3 CUP LIGHT RUM

1/3 CUP VODKA

1/4 CUP BLUE CURAÇAO

1 1/2 CUPS PINEAPPLE JUICE

1/2 CUP SOUR MIX

1/4 CUP SIMPLE SYRUP (SEE NOTE)

6 DROPS BLUE FOOD COLORING (OPTIONAL)

9 CUPS SHAVED ICE

MARASCHINO CHERRIES (1 PER CONE)

Serves 6

Hawaiian snow cones are a cross between Asian shaved ice and American snow cones. In the twenties, Japanese plantation workers in Hawaii used their machetes to shave off flakes from ice blocks, and topped them with sugar and pineapple or other tropical juices. By the fifties, the most common configuration of toppings was a rainbow of (usually three) flavors called *kalakoa*, Hawaiian for "calico."

Most mainlanders make snow cones from crunchy ice chips, and the flavoring sinks to the bottom of the cone; for this style, use the crushed ice from your freezer, or put ice cubes in a heavy-duty zip-top bag and crush them with a mallet. Hawaiian shaved ice is smooth, so it absorbs the syrups; for a true Hawaiian snow cone, shave ice cubes with a hand-cranked ice shaver or use an ice scraper to shave a large block of ice.

1. Combine all of the ingredients except the ice and cherries in a pitcher; stir well.
2. Put 1 1/2 cups of the ice in each of 6 paper cones. Pour the mixture over the ice until absorbed, top each cone with a cherry, and serve.

NOTE
To make simple syrup: Combine 2 parts water and 1 part sugar in a saucepan and bring to a boil, stirring until the sugar is dissolved. Remove from the heat and let cool. Store in a clean jar in the refrigerator for up to several weeks.

MORE HAWAIIAN SNOW CONES
Stuffed Pineapple Snow Cone: Combine 1 3/4 cups pineapple juice and 1/4 cup simple syrup in a pitcher. Put a scoop of vanilla ice cream in the bottom of each paper cone and top with 1/2 cup chopped pineapple. Put the ice on top and pour the juice mixture over the ice.

SWEET MARTINI POPS

3 TO 12 OLIVES
(½ PER POP)

5 TABLESPOONS GIN

5 TABLESPOONS SWEET VERMOUTH

⅓ CUP SUGAR

Makes 24 two-ounce ice cube–tray pops, six 8-ounce pops, or eight 6-ounce pops

Served up with flair, these *Sweet Martini Pops* glamorize afternoon luncheons. They are a classic grown-ups-only treat with style, sophistication, and flavor. Compared with actual martinis, these pops are less astringent: sweeter but still crisp. The encased olives and their transparent glow make the pops look as astounding as they taste. They are light on the vermouth and gin, so you should be able to indulge in three and get back to work.

1. In a bowl, combine the olives, gin, and sweet vermouth. Let sit for 10 minutes.
2. In a saucepan, combine 4 cups water and the sugar. Stir over low heat until the sugar is dissolved. Let cool.
3. Place 1 olive half in each pop mold or on the end of each pop stick. Add the gin mixture to the sugar water. Pour into the pop molds. Insert the sticks. Freeze for at least 12 hours.
4. Remove from the freezer; let stand at room temperature for 5 minutes before removing the pops from the molds. Feel free to dip these in some gin for an extra kick, or serve them with a shot glass half filled with gin for dipping.

ALT POPS!
Dirty Martini Pops: Replace the sweet vermouth with dry vermouth. Reduce the water to 3 cups. Add 1 cup olive juice in step 2.
Sour Apple Martini Pops: Replace the water with apple juice. Replace the gin with vodka. Replace the olives with Granny Smith apple slices. Add 6 drops green food coloring, if you like.

Opposite: These stylish pops were created in ice cube trays.
For instructions, see Mini Ice Pop Molds, page 120.

PIÑA COLADA POPS

1 CUP SHREDDED
COCONUT

STEMMED MARASCHINO
CHERRIES (1 PER POP)

2 CUPS FRESH PINEAPPLE
CUT INTO CHUNKS

2 CUPS PINEAPPLE JUICE

1 ½ CUPS COCONUT
NECTAR

1 TEASPOON PURE
VANILLA EXTRACT

½ CUP SUGAR

¼ CUP LIGHT RUM
(OPTIONAL)

*Makes 24 two-ounce
ice cube–tray pops,
six 8-ounce pops,
or eight 6-ounce pops*

Frozen into *Piña Colada Pops*, this creamy blend of coconut and pineapple is tastier than any tropical nectar. I like to make them with a big chunk of fresh pineapple and a cherry embedded right where the pop meets the stick.

1. Preheat the oven to 350 degrees F. Spread the coconut on a baking sheet and toast for 7 minutes.
2. Stick a cherry and a pineapple chunk onto the end of each pop stick.
3. Put the pineapple juice, coconut nectar, vanilla extract, sugar, and rum, if using, in a food processor or blender. Process until smooth. Stir in the toasted coconut.
4. Pour into the pop molds. Freeze for 20 minutes, or until slightly frozen. Insert the sticks. Freeze for at least 12 hours.
5. Remove from the freezer; let stand at room temperature for 5 minutes before removing the pops from the molds. If you want to play up the alcohol content, dip these in simple syrup (see page 113), then in some more light rum.

ALT POPS!
Banana Piña Colada Pops: Add 2 ripe bananas to the pineapple mixture in step 3 and puree until smooth.
Staten Island Ferry Pops: This pop honors the distinctly untropical island where I grew up. Omit the shredded coconut and coconut nectar.

BLOODY MARY POPS

2 TABLESPOONS
WORCESTERSHIRE
SAUCE

12 DROPS TABASCO
SAUCE (OR TO TASTE)

1 TEASPOON CELERY SALT

1 TEASPOON PREPARED
HORSERADISH

1/2 TEASPOON FRESHLY
GROUND BLACK PEPPER

2 1/2 CUPS TOMATO JUICE

3/4 CUP FRESH ORANGE
JUICE

3/4 CUP FRESH LEMON
JUICE

1/4 CUP VODKA

1/2 CELERY RIB, CUT
INTO VERY THIN STRIPS
(OPTIONAL)

*Makes 24 two-ounce
ice cube–tray pops,
six 8-ounce pops,
or eight 6-ounce pops*

Traditionally, Bloody Mary flavors shouldn't be savored after 6 P.M., but the fun-loving among us will ignore that dictate and enjoy these *Bloody Mary Pops* any time we please. They are delightful served with eggs, waffles, and shrimp at an early afternoon brunch.

1. In a bowl, combine the Worcestershire sauce, Tabasco sauce, celery salt, horseradish, and pepper.
2. In a pitcher, combine the tomato juice, orange juice, lemon juice, and vodka until well blended. Add the Worcestershire sauce mixture to the juice mixture.
3. Stir in the celery strips, if using.
4. Fill the pop molds with the mixture. Insert the sticks. Freeze for at least 12 hours.
5. Remove from the freezer; let stand at room temperature for 5 minutes before removing the pops from the molds. Serve to anybody who enjoys a good Bloody Mary.

ALT POPS!
Bloody Geisha Pops: Replace the vodka with sake. Omit the horseradish.

Right: Make and serve this refreshing cocktail pop in a tall shot glass.

DO-IT-YOURSELF POP MOLDS

A truly amazing feature of ice pops is that they can be cast into any shape you envision—most of them start as flavored liquids, after all. There are dozens of fabulous commercial molds available, but I encourage you to try making your own. Make simple pop molds from everyday household items, such as glasses and cookie cutters, or food packaging, like waxed paper and plastic juice boxes. Or, if you want to get really crafty, experiment with liquid silicone. Molds made from found objects or recycled materials not only display your creativity, they save space in landfills, so you can feel virtuous while enjoying your truly one-of-a-kind pops!

SIMPLE READYMADE POP MOLDS

You can make ice pop molds from any object that contains a void where liquid can be frozen. I have used everything from soap dishes, vases, and plastic bottles to beach toys, Christmas ornaments, candy packaging, and toy capsules (those little balls containing toys sold in vending machines). To start with, I suggest you follow these instructions for creating easy pop molds from everyday objects you have around the house: paper or plastic cups, waxed paper, product packaging, cookie cutters, and silicone baking molds. Once you're familiar with these techniques, look around and see what else inspires you with its pop-mold potential.

Molds Made from Cups and Glasses: Paper and plastic cups, snow cone wrappers, aluminum foil muffin cups, shot glasses, and glassware free of undercuts (grooves and curves that are smaller than the opening) can all be used to form pops. The finished pops can be served in the mold or removed before serving. Consider the presentation

possibilities before you begin: Select well-designed plastic containers or stylish glassware. I scour tag sales and flea markets for inspiring cups and glasses.

1. **To make the molds:** For some containers, all you will need to do is insert the stick from the top and freeze. When using disposable paper cups, the stick can also be inserted from the side. Cut a slit or hole in the mold for the stick. Thicker mixtures, such as pudding, ice cream, and yogurt, should not leak if the hole is close to the size of the stick. Thinner mixtures will require sealing around the stick with waterproof tape or plugging the hole with food-safe clay (available at craft supply stores).
2. **To make the pops:** Pour the pop mixture into the mold. Freeze for 20 to 30 minutes. When the mixture is partially frozen, insert the sticks so they stand upright. Freeze for at least 6 hours. When making pops in rigid molds, let the pops sit for a few minutes at room temperature to melt slightly before removing them from the molds.

Waxed Paper Molds: Waxed paper can be formed into cones, pyramids, boxes, and origami shapes to make disposable pop molds.

1. **To make the molds:** Form the paper into the desired shape and secure with duct tape. Make sure that any gaps are sealed with waterproof tape. If needed, stand the shapes upright in cups.
2. **To make the pops:** Pour the pop mixture into the mold. Freeze for 20 to 30 minutes. When the mixture is partially frozen, insert the sticks so they stand upright. Freeze for at least 6 hours.

Molds Made from Food and Product Packaging:
Water bottles, soda bottles and cans, mini milk cartons, yogurt containers, cardboard paper towel rolls, wrapping paper rolls, juice boxes, plastic baggies, candy boxes, tin cans, plastic balls, toy capsules—all of these can be recycled as super-cool ice pop molds.

1. **To make the molds:** For shapes that are not enclosed or do not have an enclosed bottom (for example, paper towel rolls), make the bottom out of rigid plastic sheet, available at hardware, art supply, and some craft stores, and attach it with a glue gun, making sure it is completely sealed. For materials that are not wax-lined, line them with waxed paper and secure with waterproof tape. Stand the shapes upright in cups if necessary.
2. **To make the pops:** Pour the pop mixture into the mold. Freeze for 20 to 30 minutes. When the mixture is partially frozen, insert the sticks so they stand upright. Freeze for at least 6 hours.

Silicone Baking Molds: Plastic cookie cutters and silicone baking molds are available in dozens of shapes. They can easily be converted into pop molds. Again, tag sales and flea markets are excellent sources for quirky cutters and molds on the cheap.

1. **To make the molds:** Insert the stick from the top or cut a tiny hole in the side with a utility knife for the stick and seal the outside with waterproof tape or food-safe clay.
2. **To make the pops:** Pour the pop mixture into the molds. Cover the tops with aluminum foil or plastic wrap and put the molds in the freezer, placing a small rock under the ends of the sticks to keep them level. Freeze for at least 6 hours. To remove the pops from the molds, push the stick toward the pop and push it up out of the mold.

A FUNNEL, A GLASS, AND A SILICONE CUPCAKE MOLD WERE USED TO MAKE THESE POPS.

MINI ICE POP MOLD

Ice cube trays of many shapes and sizes can easily be converted into mini ice pop molds. For playful, unique pops, choose trays shaped like flowers, hearts, stars, triangles, fruits, circles, or whatever other creative shapes you come across. Bonus: Mini ice pops freeze much more quickly than standard-sized pops—in just 3 to 4 hours—so if you're in a hurry, this is your pop.

To convert an ice cube tray into an ice pop mold, you need to create a lid for the tray to hold the sticks straight. Rigid plastic sheet is the best material for this, since it's reusable, easy to clean, and will last a long time. You can find it at hardware stores, art supply stores, and some craft stores. Office supply stores may sell inexpensive plastic folders you can cut apart to make the lid. Though less permanent than plastic, corrugated cardboard or chipboard covered with aluminum foil or plastic wrap also makes a perfectly serviceable lid. If you're using thinner plastic or corrugated cardboard, use a utility knife to cut rectangular slots for the sticks. If the plastic is thicker, drill holes in the lid and use wooden dowels as the sticks.

What You'll Need

- For a plastic lid: $1/8$- to $1/4$-inch-thick corrugated plastic or $1/16$- to $1/8$-inch-thick rigid plastic sheet (Styrene, PETG, or Polypropylene)
- For a cardboard lid: $1/8$- to $1/4$-inch-thick corrugated cardboard or $1/8$-inch-thick chipboard, and aluminum foil or plastic wrap to cover the cardboard
- Glue gun and glue sticks

- Ten $1 1/4$-inch binder clips per ice cube tray, $1/4$- or $3/8$-inch wooden dowels, cut to stick size, or small popsicle sticks

1. **To measure the lid:** Measure the outside rim of your ice cube tray and cut the lid material to the same size as the tray. Exact measurements will ensure a better grip when attaching binder clips.

2. **To create a spacer:** Cut 4 strips of plastic or cardboard to elevate the lid $3/8$ inch above the tray; 2 strips should be as long as the tray, 2 as wide as the tray, and they should all be as wide as the rim of the tray. Glue the spacers around the rim of the tray. Choose at least 3 locations in the center to create additional supports.

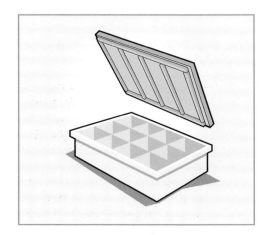

ABOVE: To keep the lid from sticking to the tray, glue $3/8$-inch-thick supports around the rim and across the center of the tray.

3. **To make a grid for stick placement:** Measure the center points of each ice cube cavity in your tray and the distance between the center points. Draw a grid on the lid to map out the center points.

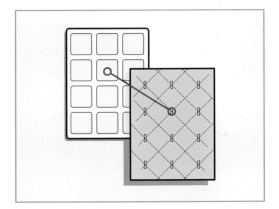

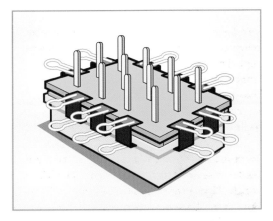

ABOVE: Use binder clips to secure the lid to the filled ice cube tray, then insert the sticks through the holes.

ABOVE: On the lid, mark where the center of each pop will be, and drill or cut holes for the sticks.

4. **To create the slots for the sticks:** If you're using dowels for sticks, use a drill to drill holes at the center points, using a drill bit the same width as the dowels. If you're using traditional pop sticks that are $7/16$ inch wide and $1/16$ inch thick, cut slits with a utility knife to that size.

5. **To fill the pop tray:** Fill the tray no more than three quarters full with the pop mixture. (The ice will expand as it freezes.) Use 2 binder clips on the short sides of the tray and 3 binder clips on the long side of the tray to hold the lid onto the tray. Insert the pop sticks or dowels and freeze for 3 to 4 hours.

6. **To remove the pops from the tray:** Remove the binder clips and lid. If the mold is silicone, the pops can be removed immediately. If the mold is hard plastic, let the pops sit at room temperature for 3 to 5 minutes before removing them from the mold.

PLASTIC BAGGIE MOLDS

Do you remember the frozen juice (that is, corn syrup and dye) sticks you begged for as a kid? You can use a food sealer, a handy kitchen appliance with a heat strip and a vacuum (available at cooking supply stores), to create healthier, more sophisticated versions of these pops. A nostalgic treat that travels well, these pops are fun to bring to potlucks and parties. Transport them in a cooler filled with ice or dry ice, and refreeze upon arrival.

What You'll Need

- Food sealer and plastic
- Funnel
- A friend, or rope and clothespins

Food sealers are kitchen appliances that are used to create bags for food storage. They have a vacuum that sucks air out of the bag and a heat strip that fuses the plastic together to seal them. For this project you will only be using the heat-sealing feature of the appliance since it is not necessary to remove the air from your pops.

1. **To prepare the bags:** Measure the length of the heat strip on the food sealer and cut a piece off the roll of plastic that is slightly smaller than the heat strip. The bag will have two open ends. Following the manufacturer's directions, heat-seal the bottom of the bag. Decide on your pop width. I usually make mine about $1^1/_4$-inch wide, but they can be any size. You will need to create two seals between each pop that are roughly $^1/_4$ inch apart. Later you will cut the

pops between these two lines. Measuring along the bottom edge of the bag, make small marks where the two seals $^1/_4$ inch apart will separate the pops. Repeat on the top edge of the bag. With the heat sealer, seal the lines in the bag.

2. **To fill the bags:** If you have a friend available, have him or her hold the bag so it is easier to fill. If you're on your own, clip the bag onto a taut rope with clothespins. Using a funnel, fill the bag with the pop mixture to roughly 2 inches from the top of the bag. This will allow room to seal the bag and for the ice to expand. Holding the bag straight, seal the top of the bag with the heat sealer about $^1/_4$ inch from the top. Cut off the excess plastic on all sides.

3. **To freeze and serve:** Freeze for 4 to 6 hours. Remove the bag from the freezer and cut the pops apart between the sealed lines. Snip off the end of a bag and squeeze the pop from the bottom to enjoy.

SILCONE POP MOLDS

You can make some incredibly imaginative pop molds with food-safe silicone. Silicone picks up detail as faint as a fingerprint and is very flexible. I use Silpak R2237S1 for my molds, but there are many other options that are also available online. The process of making a silicone mold is easy. The liquid silicone material is poured into a cup around an object. It hardens into a flexible mold. The object is taken out of the mold, and the negative space where the object had been creates a cavity for the pop mixture.

A silicone mold can be used over and over to create hundreds of ice pops. Molds can be made with multiple cavities, and several objects can be cast in the same mold, as long as there is a 3/8-inch space between them.

What You'll Need

- Found object, or object sculpted from clay, wood, or wax
- Cup or food container (paper or plastic) or pieces of cardboard to construct a box
- Glue gun and glue sticks
- Utility knife
- Raw rice
- Liquid food-safe silicone and catalyst
- Rubber bands or duct tape

1. **To decide on a pattern:** The original object shape that will be converted into a pop is called the master pattern. The pattern could be anything, such as a small toy or another found object (plastic or wood works best; glass and ceramic objects will stick to the silicone and are not practical for this purpose). You can also sculpt characters or shapes out of clay, wax, or wood to use as patterns. I use clay, which hardens so that I can easily pull it out of the silicone and use it again. Most manufactured hard plastic ice pop molds contain draft, which means they are angled slightly so you can pull the pops out easily. Consider draft when choosing your master pattern. The flexibility of silicone can accommodate small undercuts (grooves in the object), but master pattern objects that contain at least some draft are easiest to mold.

A. GOOD DRAFT: The pop will come out easily.

B. NO DRAFT: The pop will come out if it's allowed to melt slightly first.

C. BAD DRAFT: You will never get the pop out.

D. SMALL UNDERCUTS: The pop will come out with a little wiggling if the mold is made of flexible silicone.

E. LARGE UNDERCUTS: The pop will be very difficult to remove.

The simplest objects to mold have a flat side, so they'll require only a one-part mold. If there is no flat side or holes or negative spaces in the pattern, fill them with clay so the liquid silicone won't seep in.

2. **To find or make a mold container:** You'll need a paper or plastic cup, or a yogurt or other food container. $1/4$ to $3/8$ inch larger than your master pattern on all sides. More than $3/8$ inch of space around the object will only waste material and make the mold less flexible. If you cannot find an existing container that is slightly bigger than your object, construct a box out of cardboard, sealing all of the seams with a glue gun so the container doesn't leak.

3. **To make the mold:** Glue the flat side of the master pattern to the bottom of the container to keep the object from floating when you pour in the silicone. Draw a line on the container to indicate where the back of the object is positioned as a reminder, because once the silicone is poured in, you won't

ABOVE: Glue the flat side of the master pattern object to the bottom of the cup and cover it with liquid silicone. Mark a line on the cup to indicate the location of the back side of the object.

Mark a line on the hardened silicone to indicate where the back of the pattern object is. Remove or tear away the cup.

Make a cut in the silicone and remove the pattern object. Wash the mold, and it's ready for pop making!

be able to tell back from front. Later you may need to cut the mold in order to remove the object, and a cut will be less noticeable at the back.

To premeasure the silicone, pour some raw rice into the container until there is a $3/8$-inch layer of rice on top of the object. Pour the rice out into a measuring cup: This is the amount of silicone you will need. When you purchase the silicone the package will have two bottles: the silicone and the catalyst. Thoroughly mix the silicone and catalyst together to make the amount you need; they become activated

COCONUT SKULL POP   **MAI TAI TIKI POP**

and the slow hardening process begins. Pour the mixed liquid silicone around the object until it covers it by 3/8 inch. Tap the mold gently on a work surface to remove the air bubbles. (Alternatively, you can remove air bubbles by placing the mold on top of a running clothes dryer loaded with a few tennis balls for 30 minutes. Or you can put the mold on top of a stereo speaker with the bass cranked up for 30 minutes and dance until the bubbles are gone.) Then let the silicone cure for 12 to 24 hours, or as directed on the package.

When the silicone has hardened, mark a line on the hardened silicone that aligns with the line you drew on the container to indicate the back side of the object. Rip or cut the container away from the mold. The master pattern might pop right out of the mold, but if you have trouble removing the object, use a utility knife to cut a small slit in the back side of the mold to create an opening. Remove the object. Wash the mold with soap and water.

4. **To cast the ice pops:** Close the slit (if you made one) with rubber bands or duct tape. Pour the pop mixture into the mold. Freeze for 20 to 30 minutes. When the mixture is partially frozen, insert the sticks so they stand upright. Freeze for 8 hours. Remove the rubber bands or tape and remove the pop from the mold. Fabulous!

CRANBERRY KITTY POP AND LEMONY DUCK POP

ABOVE: Close up the cut in the mold by wrapping the mold with rubber bands or covering the cut with duct tape. Pour the pop mixture into the mold and partially freeze it, then insert the sticks and freeze until hard.

INDEX

Most of the photographs in this book appear on the same page or opposite the pictured recipe.
Italics in this index indicate photographs that stand alone or appear separate from their recipe.

METRIC CONVERSION CHARTS

All equivalent measurements and weights have been rounded up or down slightly.

VOLUME

U.S.	METRIC	IMPERIAL
¼ TSP	1.2 ML	
½ TSP	2.5 ML	
1 TSP	5.0 ML	
½ TBSP (1½ TSP)	7.5 ML	
1 TBSP (3 TSP)	15 ML	
¼ CUP (4 TBSP)	60 ML	2 FL OZ
⅓ CUP (5 TBSP)	75 ML	2½ FL OZ
½ CUP (8 TBSP)	125 ML	4 FL OZ
⅔ CUP (10 TBSP)	150 ML	5 FL OZ
¾ CUP (12 TBSP)	175 ML	6 FL OZ
1 CUP (16 TBSP)	250 ML	8 FL OZ
1¼ CUPS	300 ML	10 FL OZ (½ PINT)
1½ CUPS	350 ML	12 FL OZ
2 CUPS (1 PINT)	500 ML	16 FL OZ
2½ CUPS	625 ML	20 FL OZ (1 PINT)
1 QUART	1 LITER	32 FL OZ

WEIGHT

U.S.	METRIC
1 OZ	30 G
2 OZ	60 G
3 OZ	90 G
4 OZ	115 G
5 OZ	150 G
6 OZ	175 G
7 OZ	200 G
8 OZ (½ LB)	225 G
9 OZ	250 G
10 OZ	300 G
11 OZ	325 G
12 OZ	350 G
13 OZ	375 G
14 OZ	400 G
15 OZ	425 G
16 OZ (1 LB)	450 G

OVEN TEMPERATURE

OVEN MARK	F	C	GAS
VERY COOL	250–275	130–140	½–1
COOL	300	150	2
WARM	325	170	3
MODERATE	350	180	4
MODERATELY HOT	375	190	5
	400	200	6
HOT	425	220	7
	450	230	8
VERY HOT	475	250	9

LENGTH

INCHES	CENTIMETERS
¼	.65
½	1.25
1	2.5
2	5
3	7.5
4	10
5	12.5
6	15
7	17.5
8	20
9	22.5
10	25
12 (1 FT)	30